MALFEASANCE & IMMORALITY

An Analysis of the World Economic Crash of 2008,
the Corrupt Political and Financial Institutions that
Caused it, the Plan of the 1% Plutonomy
Against the 99% and Ethical Strategies
to Survive the Coming Collapse
of the Economy - A White Paper

By
Muata Ashby

Muata Ashby

THE SEMA INSTITUTE

MALFEASANCE & IMMORALITY

An Analysis of the World Economic Crash of 2008,
the Corrupt Political and Financial Institutions that
Caused it, the Plan of the 1% Plutonomy
Against the 99% and Ethical Strategies
to Survive the Coming Collapse
of the Economy - A White Paper

By
Muata Ashby

9/25/2009

http://www.egyptianyoga.com/Politics&Economics

Sema Books
P.O.Box 570459
Miami, Fl. 33257

Ashby, Muata
MALFEASANCE & IMMORALITY: An Analysis of the World Economic Crash of 2008, the Corrupt Political and Financial Institutions that Caused it and Strategies to Survive the Future Collapse of the Economy
ISBN: 978-1-937016-52-4

TABLE OF CONTENTS

INTRODUCTION

The following is a first ever publication, by the Sema Institute, of a "White Paper". The term is defined as:

> A **white paper** is an authoritative report or guide that often addresses issues and how to solve them. White papers are used to educate readers and help people make decisions. They are often used in politics and business.[i]

This paper serves as an update to the book *Dollar Crisis: The Collapse of Society and Redemption Through Ancient Egyptian Fiscal & Monetary Policy* (2008). That book was a continuation and expansion of issues presented in the book *The Collapse of Civilization and the Death of American Empire* (2006)[1]. Those books contained a detailed analysis of economic and political as well as social issues and how Maat Philosophy[ii] could offer insights into the nature of the problem, its sources and possible solutions as well as a means to develop an economic system (Fiscal and Monetary policies) that can work for all members of

---

[1] Renamed Collapse of Civilization and Death of American Empire

society. This paper contains an analysis of economic events and possible future outcomes based on those events as well as ideas individuals or groups may use in order to develop plans of action to deal with the possible detrimental events that may occur in the near and intermediate future. It serves as an update to the previous publications.

This paper is divided into two parts. The first section is a summary which contains the conclusions of each section of Part 2. This was done so that the reader may have a quick and easy understanding of what is happening with the economy and finally, the actions that should be considered to meet the challenges ahead. Then if the reader desires to see a more detailed exposition of the economic problems that are facing the United States of America and the world in general, with extensive references, they may review Part 2. For more information visit the following web site: http://www.egyptianyoga.com/Politics&Economics

Dr. Muata Ashby
The Sema Institute

PART I: Conclusions

SUMMARY

<u>BACKGROUND</u>

Many people were amazed at the dramatic rise of stocks in the late 1990's and shocked at the crash that occurred in the early 2000's. Many were also amazed at the real estate bubble that was created in the 2000's and the dramatic bursting of that economic bubble in 2008. The messages being heard in the mass media, from politicians and Wall Street executives or members of the media, that the economy is recovering and that the worst is behind us are incorrect and at worse purposely misleading. The fundamentals of the economy indicate that the economy is far from recovering but rather the opposite, it is moving towards failure because the fundamentals of the economy (consumer strength, sound currency, manufacturing base, educated population, etc.) are in dire condition. In fact, there are other massive financial and economic bubbles that are causing substantial dangers in the economy that have already and will continue to lead to further deterioration and loss of wealth. The mishandling of the economy by instituting tax cuts for the wealthy, allowing lower wages, budget deficits and now the bailouts and stimulus programs are further eroding the value of the US Dollar through inflation, a shadow tax on the lower 99% of the population. All of these issues have led to the crash of the financial system and are leading to a severe economic downturn that will cause severe stress and possible collapse of the economic system. The financial problem developed into an economic problem; the economic problem will lead to a political crisis that could produce civil strife unseen since the 1930's. These eventualities should be a serious cause of concern to anyone who has a connection to the USA economic system or it's social and or political system.

NOBODY KNEW THE CRASH WAS COMING?

Contrary to popular belief and the incorrect or false statements by politicians and others in the media, especially the financial news media, that nobody could have foreseen the events of 2008, the collapse of the stock market and the ensuing recession, etc., actually several economists, financial advisors and prominent financial institutions did know about and warned about the impending disaster. Furthermore, those same analysts who exhibited accurate foresight, have also foreseen other dire problems ahead which were caused by the past mishandling of the economy and unrestrained printing of money.

The stock market has risen between March and September 2009 but there are no fundamental reasons for the rise except the expectation of a recovery supported by illusory earnings reports facilitated by lack of inventory replacement and layoffs that artificially and temporarily inflate corporate balance sheets and the infusion of trillions of dollars to purchase and sustain the values of stocks. Such a recovery has not materialized but rather unemployment has continued to rise and wages have continued to stay flat or go down. There can be no recovery while wages are down and unemployment is rising. The USA economy has to produce at least 130,000 new jobs just to absorb the new people moving into the economy every year. Last month (Sep. 2009) 263,000 jobs were lost. Since the economy started to slide downward in the Fall of 2007 (recession) over 7 million people have lost their jobs. These factors and others continue to be ignored in the media and by prominent financial advisors, the same ones who, in 2007 and early 2008, were saying that there was no problem with the economy.

FRAUDULENT STOCK MARKET AND CORRUPT ECONOMIC SYSTEM

The economic system of the USA and other western countries is supposedly based on a "Capitalist philosophy" which also supposedly adheres to the ideal of "Free Markets". This section explains why the economic system is in reality not a capitalistic system because capitalism is a failed economic model. It also explains why in reality there are no free markets. Furthermore, it explains in detail the vast fraud that has and is being perpetrated on the general population which makes the exploits of Bernard Madoff, the investment advisor who stole more than $50 Billion is actually not the only Ponzi scheme in the USA economy; the USA economic system itself operates largely as a Ponzi scheme to benefit the largest corporations and institutions. The fraud that led to the crash of the economy in the Fall of 2008 was perpetrated through manipulation of markets and through manipulation of the tax code and wage system in order to favor the wealthy segments of the population. Trillions of dollars have been misappropriated and used to prop up undeserving corporations as well as institutions representing the wealth of a minority of the population through bailouts and other subsidies. Actually, the USA stock market and indeed the economy as a whole, from the beginning but especially since 1980, may be likened to a Ponzi scheme[2] and a pyramid[3] scheme set up in such a way as to take funds from the masses to transfer that wealth to the top 1% of the population. The USA economic system has been set up in such a way that the USA borrows moneys from its citizens and from other countries by selling bonds to them. Then the government spends the moneys on non-productive items and perishables, expecting that the growth in the economy or some future generation will be able to pay for it. The massive debts of the USA government are so massive now that it cannot be paid. This is causing the failure of the economy and the loss of confidence by investors in the currency of the USA. In this section we present a confidential memo from the largest bank group in the world to their wealthy customers which expressed the philosophy of the wealthy and acknowledges the fact that the wealthy have created a society where the

---

[2] A **pyramid scheme** is a non-sustainable business model that involves the exchange of money primarily for enrolling other people into the scheme, often without any product or service being delivered.

[3] A **Ponzi scheme** is a fraudulent investment operation that pays returns to separate investors from their own money or money paid by subsequent investors, rather than from any actual profit earned. The Ponzi scheme usually offers returns that other investments cannot guarantee in order to entice new investors, in the form of short-term returns that are either abnormally high or unusually consistent. The perpetuation of the returns that a Ponzi scheme advertises and pays requires an ever-increasing flow of money from investors in order to keep the scheme going.

wealthy get a disproportionate amount of the wealth. The economic imbalances and the greed of such an arrangement have led to unbridled and unprecedented economic deficits, public and private debt and devastating losses in the manufacturing base. These detriments to the economy, a kind of devastation of the fundamentals of the economy have produced a situation in which the economy will not be able to recover from its current condition for several years and that also not without radical changes that will be politically unpalatable to the ordinary citizen.

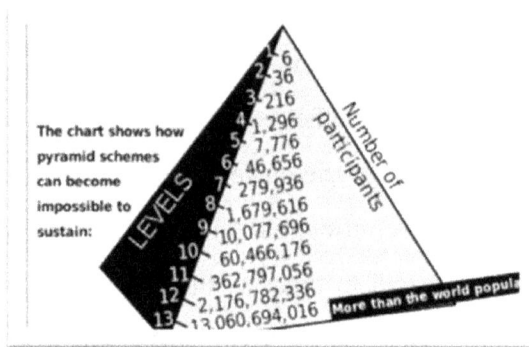

The chart shows how pyramid schemes can become impossible to sustain:

LEVELS
1
2 - 6
3 - 36
4 - 216
5 - 1,296
6 - 7,776
7 - 46,656
8 - 279,936
9 - 1,679,616
10 - 10,077,696
11 - 60,466,176
12 - 362,797,056
13 - 2,176,782,336
- 13,060,694,016

Number of participants

More than the world population

GIVEN THE AFORESAID, WHAT CAN WE EXPECT IN THE NEAR AND INTERMEDIATE TERM?

There are presently TWO imminent major dangers ahead and one other factor in the near future that will likely push the economy into a massive and protracted cyclical downward trend

Based on the current condition of the economy there are two main problems facing the USA and countries experiencing similar economic conditions. Firstly, since the recent economic activity in the stock market (upon which the economy is partially dependent) has been based on an illusory concept, that the economy can be lifted by simply raising the price of stocks in the stock market, there is a danger of another crash of the stock market on the order of what happened in the Fall of the year 2008. This would mean a massive loss of wealth for all and a loss of confidence in the economy that could trigger a deflationary depression. Prices of stocks and other assets would go down again but also wages would go down further since there would be more massive layoffs and business failures, bankruptcies, foreclosures, etc. This eventuality may happen in a short period of time or over a period of a few years and would lead the economy into a deeper recession if not depression. Such an possibility could lead to breakdown in the social order and even the possibility of the imposition of martial law and the suspension of the constitution.

Secondly, due to the massive deficits and overprinting of money as well as the deterioration of the productive base in the economy, the currency of the USA will likely deteriorate further. This might occur quickly or over a period of years but it has already begun. If the currency continues to fail it would mean loss of buying power of the US Dollar and everything denominated in dollars. Everything could cost more in terms of dollars but each dollar would buy less than before. This would lead to a further downward shock on the economy and even precipitate a crash or protracted decline of the economy as a whole. The current US Dollar buys only 3% of what the US Dollar of 1913 could buy. This is due to inflation caused by malfeasance and a fractional banking system that has been designed to produce debt and money out of thin air.[iii]

If either or both of these scenarios occurs it will mean a loss of wealth and buying power, instant "pooring" of those who own dollars or assets related to dollars. It could lead to loss of lifestyle, loss of services, bankruptcy of the government and personal bankruptcy as well. This is a threat to the financial wellbeing of everyone but also a threat to one's capacity to lead a life in an environment of safety, peace and security.

Along with the issues listed above there is another factor that will likely push the economy into a downward cyclical pattern, the retirement of the baby boomer generation.

What to do about the TWO main dangers right now?

There are still some strategies that can be applied to avoid or at least mitigate the effects of the problems listed above. There are strategies to deal with the problem of a crashing economy and its aftermath, a collapsing economy. There are strategies to deal with the issue of a falling currency. For more on these strategies the reader is directed to this section of PART 2 where they will find a more detailed description of the actions that should be taken. Clearly, the path that the USA government and economy are on now is pointing towards decline and probable collapse. This means that it is prudent to seek legal methods to secure wealth and prepare for hard times in which the economy will be depressed for a prolonged period of time. This means providing for one's income, safety and security as far as one's living situation and asset preservation. See the section entitled: What to do about the TWO main dangers right now?

PART 2: ANALYSIS

BACKGROUND

Since the Fall of 2005 I have been looking into the subject of economics as it relates to ancient history and modern history. I discovered some disturbing information that allowed us to foresee the economic recession that started in summer 2007 and the financial crash started in the Fall of 2008.

We have further and updated information that points to possible negative economic conditions ahead so I thought I would share some further analysis and an update on possible scenarios for the future. If a possible disaster does not come to pass you lose nothing by listening and preparing but by doing so you will be prepared in such an eventuality and if it does not occur you will be more economically wealthier regardless.

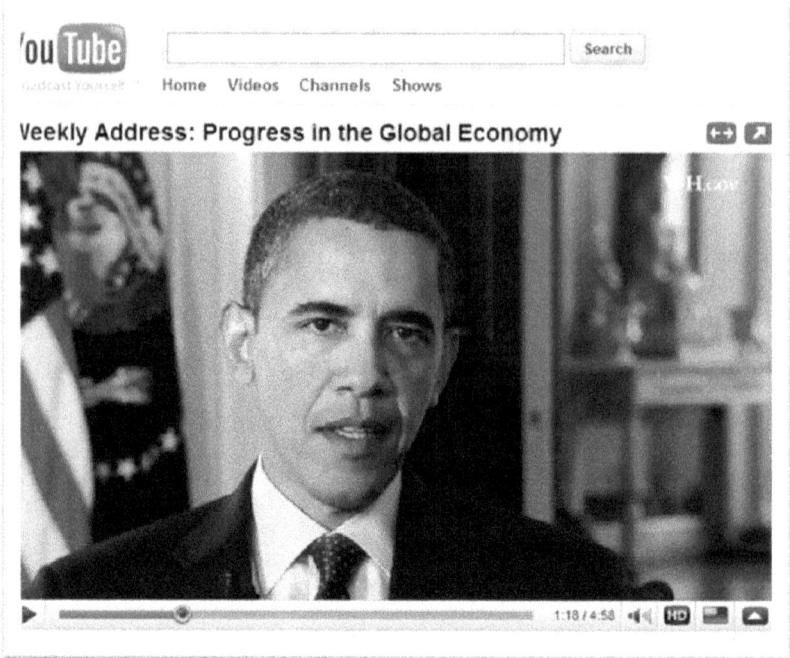

Weekly Address: Progress in the Global Economy

What you have been hearing on the news and talk shows recently, from people like the head of the Federal Reserve (Ben Bernanke) that "From a technical perspective, the recession is very likely over at this point,"[iv] and President Obama, that "we've stopped our economic free fall",[v] is wishful thinking and nothing more. Remember, the same people who created the de-regulatory environment (Robert Rubin, Larry Summers, Ben Bernanke, Tim Geithner and others) that allowed the current economic conditions to develop and who were saying, in 2007[vi], that there was nothing wrong with the housing market or the economy are still in charge and advising the president and are now saying we are past the disaster. The fundamentals of the economy do not support that assessment of the situation. Why? Briefly:[vii]

1. Mainstream political, corporate and economic leaders are operating under false concepts which are part of a larger ideology referred to as Capitalism. The false concepts have been compounded by malfeasance and corruption of lawmakers in collusion with corporate leaders but prolonged past their failing point through market manipulations and by the world currency reserve status of the US Dollar. The false ideas are:[viii]

a. Debt does not matter

b. Government can be trusted to manage the country's currency (without overprinting)

c. The value of the dollar on foreign exchanges does not matter

d. Gold is an anachronism that has no role in a modern economy

2. The fundamental segments (pillars) of the economy (consumer strength, sound currency, manufacturing base, educated population, etc.) have suffered purposeful deterioration due to:

a. creating an imbalance between rich and poor,

i. through reduction of wages and tax cuts for the rich over the last 30 years

1. NOTE: wage reduction can occur through an outright cut in the amount of a paycheck or

2. wage reduction occurs more frequently through inflation.

a. A worker may receive more money (ex. 10% raise) but inflation has increased 15% so their wages have actually gone down. The workers can feel they are doing better because they are receiving more dollars but that is an illusion.

b. This problem is easier to understand if we note that gold always maintains the same relative value to the dollar. An ounce of gold purchased the same amount of valuables 30 years ago as it can today in terms of dollars

b. creating national debt (now 12 trillion and increasing),

c. allowing the health care industry to steal wealth from the general population,

d. wars of conquest,

e. artificially low interest rates, inflationary creation of money,

f. allowing the rampant mortgage fraud perpetrated by banks (*subprime mortgages, derivatives, currency default swaps, etc.*) and the real estate bubble of the mid 2000's to be created, even though the Federal Bureau of Investigation alerted the Justice department as to the rampant mortgage fraud that was being perpetrated not by borrowers but by banks. When the bubble burst in 2008 president Bush and the congress allowed the removal of white collar crime FBI investigators from the investigations.

g. comingling 401 K's and IRA's of private individuals and private pension funds with funds of commercial banks with investment banks (or allowing Wall Street big banks to risk public and private funds)

h. allowing investment banks to make Las Vegas style bets not with their own money but with the people's moneys (with the consent of both political parties, spearheaded by the democratic party president Bill Clinton, and Alan Greenspan of the Federal Reserve (Central Bank of the USA) and Wall Street Executives), an supported by republican party politicians, specifically to allow unbridled financial speculation and financial economic activity (shifting the economy from manufacturing to service economy-financial activity is paper and financial instruments instead of real investment and production of valuable goods (produce financial instruments instead of real goods like cars and washing machines-manufacturing)).

i. the creation of a tech bubble in the late 1990's and the real estate bubble in the mid 2000's and allowing the creation of *Derivatives,* and the selling of *Credit Default Swaps* (toxic financial securities that were not only worthless but were a scam to sell garbage financial instruments around the world that stole the wealth of individuals and institutions around the world and caused the collapse of credit markets (along with the defaults on the subprime mortgages)).

The varied areas of malfeasance listed above led to the recession (economic slow down) that began in 2007 and the crash of Fall 2008 which will likely be followed by an economic depression. These problems listed above, and others, have not been resolved by the bailouts of financial institutions (banking and related corporations) or stimulus packages supposedly aimed at getting people to spend money since those efforts only produce temporary results while the underlying problems of the economy are not being addressed. One year after the supposedly greatest economic disaster since the Great Depression saw no enactment of new regulations to address the crisis. Those failed efforts (bailouts and stimulus packages) will continue to prolong the negative developments in the economy and prevent recovery as they are adding more problems, deficits, insolvency and delaying the actions that should be taken to fix the economy while allowing people who do not have as much resources to expend what they have while hoping for an economic recovery only to end up broke while at the beginning they may have just been poor or unemployed. ALL countries, in the past, that have taken the action of leaving a gold standard, adopted deficits and have engaged in printing money without restriction, bailed out bankrupt companies and institutions, promoted a disparity wherein the rich get richer and the poor get poorer, have ended up with an economy that cannot grow because the majority of the people are poor, the economy becomes bankrupt, the currency is blown up and hyper inflated. A gold standard keeps an economy in check because governments could not over tax the people, overinflate the currency, run large deficits or engage in expenditures without savings. Going off the gold standard allowed the USA government to engage in unbridled borrowing and spending, fielded by other countries buying USA debt and sustained by the world reserve currency status of the US Dollar. So the buildup of the economy of the USA since leaving the gold Standard in 1971 under President Nixon, was not due to wealth but do to debt. The debt has reached a level that cannot be reversed politically or economically. No politician wants to tell the USA population that taxes must go up and services must go down so the debt can be paid. That would be political suicide because other politicians would say otherwise and people would want to believe those who say we can continue like this indefinitely. Also, politicians would not want to give up the ability to print money out of thin air because money is power. To clarify, when the term "out of thin air" is used, this means that the Federal Reserve writes checks but there is no money in the bank; the check itself brings money into existence by just saying it exists.

"When the Federal Reserve writes a check for a government bond it does exactly what any bank does, it creates money, it created money purely and simply by writing a check."[ix]

3. as of 10/4/2009 unemployment was still rising because businesses still cannot support sufficient economic activity because consumers do not have moneys to spend, as many have lost their jobs and the real estate bubble, caused by people being given moneys for real estate loans (home equity loans) that were not supported by the true value of the home, has stopped. The downturn in the economy has led to unemployment, bankruptcies and foreclosures that also mean lower taxes collected so the government's ability to pay down it's debts is further diminished (the deficits and bailouts) so it needs to raise taxes, cut services and borrow more and that means more printing of money out of thin air which adds to inflationary pressures on the currency and economy. This also means a further decline in the Gross Domestic Product (GDP) of the country and

constitutes further incapacity to pay the liabilities of the country.

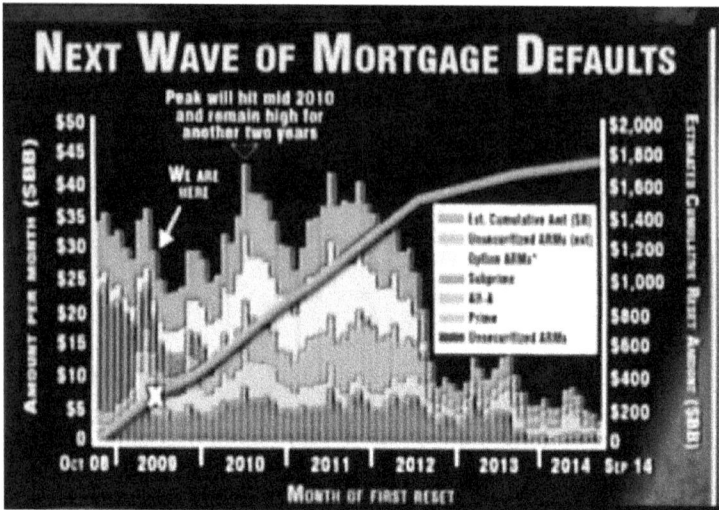

4. as of 10/4/2009 residential foreclosures were still rising; banks are not reporting the losses so as to avoid having to list the losses on their balance sheets. There are two more waves of subprime mortgage failures ---like what happened between summer 2007 and fall 2008---that will hit the economy in 2010-2012. As more foreclosures hit the economy this will further depress consumer's capacity to spend and that will depress businesses and a spiraling cycle of economic depression can develop further and deeper. This will spark commercial real estate failures and bankruptcies. This process of decline has already started. [x]

5. The downturn in the economy has forced subprime mortgages (from borrowers who could not afford the mortgage and should not have been given a mortgage of this size in the first place) into foreclosure but is now also forcing a large number of prime mortgages (from borrowers who could afford to pay the mortgage payment) into foreclosure as well because many people with "good" jobs have lost their jobs or have entered bankruptcy due to medical bills or other related problems due to the downturn in the economy.
(http://www.cnn.com/video/#/video/business/2009/08/20/d cl.christie.foreclosures.cnn?iref=videosearch)

6. the actions of the government –first knowingly creating the bubble economy- trying to create perpetual "good times" based on printing money and allowing the rich to benefit from economic activity based on mortgage derivatives (financial instruments (securities) based on mortgages to people who could not afford them (subprime mortgages))- and trying to later bail out banks and financial institutions (that made toxic loans knowingly and packaged them and sold them around the world –the same banks that should have been allowed to go bankrupt or put up their own moneys from their sales to bail themselves out) has made

the already bad condition of the US dollar worse which will bring higher inflation which will make the economic situation for the average person worse.

7. Due to malfeasance and the irrational ideological defense of a pseudo capitalist system which is in reality corporate socialism, or more specifically, corporate welfare at public expense and exploitation of workers, the USA economy faces unprecedented debt which has led to insolvency and has already and will continue to lead to the further devaluation of the US dollar. Tax cuts for the rich (especially under Reagan and Bush) and purposeful reduction in real wages over the last 35 years (the Chairman of the Federal Reserve (Alan Greenspan) admitted this openly) are demonstrations of willful and purposeful maintenance of the general population and workers as poor and subservient members of society.[xi] This practice is a prime contributor to the degradation of the economy, as workers who have low wages cannot support the economy. The Federal Reserve compensated for this problem by extending low interest money to commercial banks that gave out credit cards and low interest loans especially for second mortgages so that people who had equity in their homes could take it out and spend it. This

was not real wealth but the creation of debt, thus causing the country to have not only massive government debt but also massive private debt (of individuals).

8. Many people have compared the present situation to the "Great Depression" of the 1930's but this is not an apt comparison. The present situation is potentially much worse because:

a. In the 1930's people did not have so much credit card debt.

b. In the 1930's people did not have second mortgages because most people did not own homes.

c. In the 1930's the government did not have the overwhelming national debt but rather budget surpluses.

d. In the 1930's the country had a strong manufacturing base, now it is minimal.

e. In the 1930's the USA economy had trade surpluses and not trade deficits.

The above is not a detailed or exhaustive list of all of the problems but they are the main and imminent problems.

NOBODY KNEW THE CRASH WAS COMING?

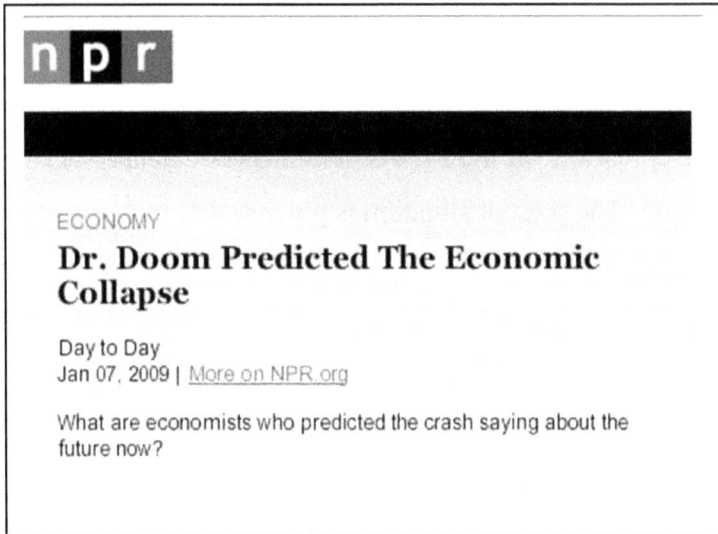

n p r

ECONOMY

Dr. Doom Predicted The Economic Collapse

Day to Day
Jan 07, 2009 | More on NPR.org

What are economists who predicted the crash saying about the future now?

Contrary to the President's and newscaster's, saying that nobody could have known the financial collapse was coming, these problems were foreseen and warned about by certain independent economists and financial advisors (www.dougfabian.com, www.trendsresearch.com, www.moneyandmarkets.com, www.mcalvany.com) that are not tied to the system that is dependent on selling garbage to the public to sustain bubble economies and unwise investments that only serve financial advisors and companies that sell junk financial instruments – like Lehman Brothers, Goldman Sacks, Chase, Citigroup, etc. and only benefit those companies and their wealthy owners as well as those who finance and sell the junk. In short, the US economy and stock markets in particular are not on a level playing field.[xii] If the coming economic collapse was known about by economists, private financial advisors and prominent organizations like Standard & Poors (see below), before it began, it follows that the government and corporate leaders did little to rectify the situation and warn of the problem but rather allowed the public to continue spending and not preparing for the looming disaster. This willful negligence by government leaders and business leaders further compounded the losses while allowing themselves to remain in positions of power and in positions to continue profiting.

> ### *Experts of Standard & Poor's forecast a global economic collapse.*
> The collapse will be caused with the demise of the US dollar rate against the European currency by more than 30 percent. The dollar, specialists say, may lose almost 45 percent of its current value against the euro. The European Central Bank has expressed its concerns with the forecast from Standard & Poor's. The European financial specialists say that the demise of American currency will endanger the global economy on the whole.
> **Pravda Online**, Wednesday, February 01, 2006.[xiii]

Donnerstag, 1. Oktober 2009, 20:31 Uhr

Dow Jones Deutschland

Nachrichten ▾ : English : Unternehmens-Center : Video : RSS & Newsletter : Arc

English

World Bank President Sees Other Reserve Currency Options To Dollar

28.09.09, 19:48 Uhr | Lesezeichen | Versenden

WASHINGTON -(Dow Jones)- Calling for a coordinated effort to rebalance the global economy and power structure in the wake of the economic crisis, World Bank President Robert Zoellick said Monday that the dollar could increasingly lose its status as the dominant reserve currency in a multi-polar world. (photo: ddp)

Zoellick, in prepared remarks for a wide-ranging speech on the causes and implications of the crisis, said the dollar would remain a "major currency," but that it would likely face competition as a reserve currency.

The continuing fall of the USA economy and currency has prompted governments around the world to call for an alternative world reserve currency to the US Dollar.[xiv] Every year more business and commerce is conducted in currencies other than the dollar, so the process of reducing the US Dollar as the reserve world currency has been occurring. The loss of world currency status would severely curtail the capacity of the US economy to take advantage of the economic advantage of having the world's reserve currency would have severe effects on the US economy; among the main benefits lost are: A-automatic increased demand for the dollar that the *reserve currency status* creates. B-The country of the reserve currency can export its malfeasance to the world (Ex. Inflation). C- Easier to run higher trade deficits with greatly postponed economic impact.

However, as we can see, with the current economic crisis, the impact is postponed but not deferred forever. D-the USA runs a perpetual trade deficit because the USA does not have sufficient products to sell to the world (The USA buys more than it sells). The other countries accept dollars because they can buy other things with it from other countries where it is accepted. If the dollar ceases to be the world reserve currency this arrangement will stop. The USA economy will remain isolated. Since there is little produced in the USA all imports will cost much more since other countries will want to be paid in other currencies besides the US Dollar; their currencies will have risen versus the dollar.

FRAUDULENT STOCK MARKET AND CORRUPT ECONOMIC SYSTEM

Will Bernanke's Secret Debt Solution End The Financial Crisis?
UncommonWisdomDaily.com

Dick & Sharon's LA PROGRESSIVE

HOME   ABOUT US   CALENDAR   VIDEO NEWS   STORE   CONTACT US   SUPPORT US   AU

Home » Economic Justice

Bloomberg Sues The Fed For Disclosure

by Charley James posted on Thursday, 13 November 2008   2 Comments

— by Charley James —

Lost in the wake of Henry Paulson's announcement Wednesday that Treasury is "changing direction" in how it doles out money in the bank rescue plan is a little-noticed lawsuit filed last Friday by Bloomberg LP, the business news wire service. It is suing the Federal Reserve Board's governors for public records that would answer two simple questions: Who is receiving $2 trillion in Fed loans and what collateral are taxpayers getting to support them?

Wall Street and the financial system of the USA economy is not unlike a Ponzi and or pyramid scheme whereby financial executives (insiders) in collusion with the media at the top collaborate to take moneys from ordinary investor's stocks, mutual funds, 401Ks and IRAs at the bottom (selling company stocks regardless of what the financial condition of the company is (http://www.youtube.com/watch?v=Vi6bxKAAHzQ&featu re=quicklist) and or stolen through market manipulation. Wall Street sells financial instruments which are toxic (worthless or destroy net worth) and then absconds with the proceeds while those who bought the toxic financial instruments later discover they are worthless or worse. Market manipulation was described by Jim Kramer (famous "financial news" commentator (salesman for Wall Street)) as "shenanigans" to "control" the market. He admitted that he and others manipulated the market through spreading lies about other companies and spending moneys to manipulate the price of mutual funds or the stock of other companies to inflate stocks, get regular people to buy them and then undercut the stock to take the value from those who have bought into it (http://www.youtube.com/watch?v=HRa0B34jMOQ); he said that the mechanics of market manipulation are more important than economic fundamentals" (being able to manipulate is more important than ordinary trading and the real valuations—because those can be manipulated). While this may not have been "illegal" due to collusion with Washington lawmakers who allowed and continue to allow such practices, it was and is unethical and immoral but immorality presupposes a person had morals to begin with so perhaps it should be thought of as amoral and if the stock market is amoral then what can we expect of an economic system centered in it? Goldman Sacks, the most powerful of the investment banks and leaders in the creation of the toxic *derivative mortgage securities* and *Credit Default Swaps,* that led to the present economic crisis, announced that they lost a computer program that could be used to manipulate the economic markets! Are we to assume that Goldman Sacks was not manipulating markets with this same computer program? (http://www.bloomberg.com/apps/news?pid=20601039&si d=aFeyqdzYcizc)

Homeowners frustrated by mortgage assistance program

STORY HIGHLIGHT:
- CNN told numerou
- Making Home Affor
- Treasury: 230,000

updated 12:21 p.m. EDT, Tue September 1, 2009

Next Article in Politic

READ   VIDEO

By Jessica Yellin
CNN National Political Correspondent

(CNN) -- The Obama administration's Making Home Affordable program was designed to help homeowners like Mark Kollar and Angela Baca-Kollar keep their homes.

When the recession hit, the Arizona couple's income plummeted. They tried everything they could think of to hold on to their house. They drained their savings account, sold their 401(k), changed jobs.

It wasn't enough, and foreclosure is set to begin in a week.

The Kollars thought they had one last hope: the Making Home Affordable program, which should have reduced their monthly mortgage to affordable payments. In theory, it'd be a win-win: The Kollars and their two children keep their home, and the nation avoids one more foreclosure.

Mark Kollar and Angela Baca-Kollar took part in the Making Home Affordable program

The problem? The bank hasn't been playing along, and the Kollars have no place to turn.

It is important to note that the financing system of the USA economy (Wall Street Banks and the Federal Reserve[xv]) is a sham and was not set up to benefit the people in general but rather Wall Street and it's owners (who also happen to give contributions (legalized bribery) to Washington congress people, the president and the judiciary officials). The Federal Reserve did not stabilize the economy, the purpose for which it was supposedly created. Rather, it has presided over various market crashes and now two great depressions while at the same time leading the US dollar to lose 97% of the value it had when the Federal Reserve began operations. However, the real economy of real people who need goods is not a sham in terms of the fact that ordinary people legitimately need food, vehicles, clothing, and other real goods. However, that process of economic activity (real economy) is distorted by the actions of the wealthy that can control lawmakers and manipulate markets. Also, the rampant consumerism is destructive because even that is based on a premise of overconsumption that is detrimental to the environment and thus eventually unsustainable; that consumption is promoted so that corporations can make more profits regardless of the consequences. It is important to note that markets can only be manipulated to a certain extent and then market forces (fundamentals) cannot be contained – so eventually bailouts and other manipulative schemes will fail and the economy will collapse no matter what schemes are attempted. In the present day economies of the countries that profess to be capitalistic, the concept of "Free Markets" and "Capitalism" is a hoax,[xvi] a slogan for general consumption while the reality is that there are no free markets but rather manipulated ones, manipulated by the state which is controlled by *plutocracies*.[xvii] Plutocracies convert even democratic government and economic systems into Crony Capitalism. Crony Capitalism is a system in which the masses are taxed, their wages are not allowed to go up and economic risk is shifted to them so that rich speculators can use the wealth of the country and never worry because they will be bailed out if their businesses fail. In Crony Capitalism the corporations receive preference so that the wealthy, who run the corporations or who can invest in them, may become more wealthy and powerful. Crony Capitalism is what western economies are based on. Crony Capitalism may be thought of as a government/economic partnership whereby a centrally managed economy is developed in such a manner so that a small group of insiders are able to covertly subsidize themselves at the expense of the outsiders (the public). An example of that kind of subsidy is government officials giving *no bid contracts*[xviii] to people they know. Not "bailing out" ordinary people[xix] such as with mortgage foreclosure assistance programs that do not work, while at the same time giving bailouts to companies that are

Sept. 21, 2003

All In The Family

Company Official Defends No-Bid Army Contract

By Rebecca Leung

Font size   Print   Share

HALLIBURTON

PHOTO
Vice President Dick Cheney was the former CEO of Halliburton. (AP / CBS)

INTERACTIVE
Battle For Iraq
The government, the insurgency, key players, background and photos.

(CBS) Almost as soon as the last bomb was dropped over Iraq, the United States began the business of rebuilding the country. As it turns out, it's very big business.

The U.S. will spend approximately $25 billion to repair Iraq by the end of next year - and billions will be needed after that.

Almost all of that money will go to private contractors who vie for lucrative government deals to rebuild Iraq's roads, retrain its police force and operate its airports.

Given all the taxpayer money involved, you might think the process for awarding those contracts would be open and competitive.

But, as 60 Minutes reported last spring, the earliest contracts were given to a few favored companies. And some of the biggest winners in the sweepstakes to rebuild Iraq have one thing in common: lots of very close friends in very high places. Correspondent Steve Kroft reports.

One is Halliburton, the Houston-based energy services and construction giant whose former CEO, Dick Cheney, is now vice president of the United States.

Even before the first shots were fired in Iraq, the Pentagon had secretly awarded Halliburton subsidiary Kellogg, Brown & Root a two-year, no-bid contract to put out oil well fires and to handle other unspecified duties involving war damage to the country's petroleum industry. It is worth up to $7 billion.

supposedly "too big to fail because their closing would hurt the economy," is a form of crony capitalism. Collaboration between the wealthy to give each other opportunities while preventing ordinary people from achieving economic success primarily through assigning risk and applying taxation disproportionately, and or restricting educational and business opportunities to particular groups or families (oligarchy) or a particular ethnic and social class (the wealthy of a ruling class (plutocracy) who can afford advanced college degrees and who are connected to other persons of wealth) is a form of cronyism. Capitalism is a failed concept for sustainable economy because it would ultimately lead to a monopoly of one company owning everything since stronger companies would take the business away from others or buy them out; yet the supposed ideal of capitalism in which insolvent and inefficient companies should be allowed to fail so that better run companies can take their place is not followed by government and corporate leaders, the main proponents of Capitalism. They enact laws to prevent too much consolidation of business because they know that if it goes too far it will develop into an unsustainable situation where the corporation would take over government itself. That one company would have a monopoly and set any price for all products essentially relegating everyone to not just a position of powerless consumers but de facto peasants who owe their property and very existence and welfare to the corporation and are subject to its whims. So, contrary to the supposed ideal of capitalism, many companies have been granted bailouts by the government when they supposedly had financial difficulties. Therefore, it would seem that bailouts subvert the supposed ideal of Capitalism in the view of its supposed proponents (corporate leaders and free market ideologues). So capitalism is not being practiced even though television pundits and political or corporate leaders tout the benefits of capitalism and how 'it built' the country. In reality, stolen lands from Native Americans,

Slave labor from Africans, usurping natural resources of Africa, the Americas and Asia, the exploitation of peoples of the Far East and Australia and investment from the rich of Europe were responsible for the building up of the economies of western countries. So, the rich corporations and the wealthy, while extolling the virtues of capitalism, do not reject bailouts even as they argue against tax cuts and stimulus packages for the lower economic classes (middle class, and the poor). This activity reveals the mendacity of Capitalism's proponents and adherents. A salient example of Crony Capitalism was when, during the height of the financial crisis in the Fall of 2008, the USA Central Bank, the Federal Reserve, gave out two TRILLION dollars to undisclosed corporations. They refused to disclose the names of the recipients and were sued. Upon losing the suit they still refused to disclose the information. Many people have faith in the ideal of democracy, government by the people; however, they do not realize that real and direct democracy was never the intent of the founding fathers of the United States of America, despite their lofty rhetoric about "We the people," "a more perfect union", "establish justice", "promote the general welfare", etc.[xx] Rather, the ideal of "democracy" as they might have envisioned it, was subverted by their own efforts to make government more opaque and unequal, favoring white men land owners and reducing women and people of color to servants and slaves.

FINANCIAL SENSE NEWSHOUR

With Jim Puplava

Catherine Austin Fitts
Founder & President of Solari, Inc.

America's Black Budget and the Manipulation of Mortgage & Financial Markets
May 22nd, 2004

Select the Audio Format
Transcription Real Player Mp3

As President of Solari, Inc., Catherine is currently spearheading the Solari Circles Campaign to help make healthy local living economies the best investment worldwide.

Catherine previously served as Managing Director and Member of the Board of Directors of the Wall Street investment bank, Dillon, Read & Co., Inc. She also served as Assistant Secretary of Housing/Federal Housing Commissioner at HUD in the first Bush Administration, and was the President and Founder of Hamilton Securities Group, Inc., a broker-dealer/investment bank and software developer that successfully completed $12 billion of transactions and $500 billion of portfolio strategy prototyping the solari model. Catherine has a BA from the University of Pennsylvania, an MBA from The Wharton School, and studied Chinese at the Chinese University of Hong Kong. Catherine serves on the advisory board of Sanders Research Associates in London, and publishes the column Mapping the Real Deal in Scoop Media in New Zealand

The USA government was set up as a republic, a representative system which allows representatives to act on other's behalf or act of their own accord or based on parameters other than from those who elected them. So even when a politician is voted in with an overwhelming mandate that person can still subvert the wishes of the people and even break the laws whilst only suffering the punishment of being voted out at the time of the next elections. Such a system, whereby the people have no recourse but to accept criminal or otherwise unwanted politicians for the duration of their terms in office, facilitates those in power to replace government officials who have been disgraced or have lost favor with the electorate with more appealing candidates that in reality serve the power elite of the population should not be referred to as democracy but plutocracy since the plutocrats control government and not the people. In other words, the promise of democracy in such a system is a hoax. Thus, the original ideal of democracy has been "hollowed out"[xxi] and replaced with corrupt 'free market economics' such that free market economics, a system of capitalist control of markets while euphemistically calling them 'free' is supported at the expense of the people. The people of the country with the Crony Capitalist politico/economic system as well as the masses of people where 'free markets' are opened up, are taken advantage of, exploited and their resources are taken to supply the endless overconsumption that is ravaging peoples lives and the environment, but which sustains profit-making enterprises for Crony Capitalists. Crony Capitalism is supported, therefore, by politicians who are supposedly empowered to look after the peoples wellbeing but who instead protect the interests of corporations and the wealthy. This arrangement is called *Fascism* (collusion between government and corporations to run and control government for the benefit of corporations and the wealthy). Those who have become rich through this manipulation have not done so through "fair" means and the playing field is not level but tilted in favor of the wealthy, powerful and connected –the manipulation has taken the form of stimulation of the economy in the 1980s by deregulation, large deficits, baby boomer cash, and financial sophistication (derivatives, securitization, globalization, etc.) –all unfair, unsustainable, inflationary (market grows out of proportion with its fundamentals into a bubble (false) economy) and unethical but also all expedient. In recent years the manipulation has taken the form of misappropriation of *TRILLIONS* of dollars from Federal funds (public funds) to covertly control supposedly free markets,[xxii] the value of the US Dollar and the value of gold.

New User? Sign Up | Sign in | Help   Get Yahoo! Toolbar

YAHOO! FINANCE   Search

HOME   INVESTING   NEWS & OPINION   PERSONAL FINANCE   MY PORTFOLIOS   TEC

Get Quotes   Finance Search

Scottrade $7 Online Trades   AMERITRADE   Scottrade ELITE

Federal Reserve Admits Hiding Gold Swap Arrangements, GATA Says

Business Wire

Press Release
Source: Gold Anti-Trust Action Committee Inc
On Wednesday September 23, 2009, 9:30 am EDT

Buzz up! 68   Print

MANCHESTER, Conn.--(BUSINESS WIRE)--The Federal Reserve System has disclosed to the Gold Anti-Trust Action Committee Inc. that it has gold swap arrangements with foreign banks that it does not want the public to know about.

The disclosure, GATA says, contradicts denials provided by the Fed to GATA in 2001 and suggests that the Fed is indeed very much involved in the surreptitious international central bank manipulation of the gold price particularly and the currency markets generally.

This is the current state of the US economy and its legacy as well as the source of its own corruption and eventual likely downfall.

Thus, off book public funds have been used behind the scenes to control economic markets at the same time that quasi governmental institutions like the Federal Reserve and businesses such as Goldman Sacks, in collusion with the Treasury department and the Federal Reserve, have taken unfair advantages by manipulating markets through special computer programs and supercomputers which are directly connected to trading exchanges in order to preempt and subvert ordinary investors. Mussolini and the Fascists of Italy in the early 20th century saw what they called the birth of Supercapitalism, (in the USA and other European countries) the last stage in the development of an economic system (capitalism) wherein those who control the means of production control the wealth of a society. Supercapitalism is a form of decadent capitalism and is the degenerate and final form which is characterized by *overconsumption;*[xxiii] the over consumption leads the state to promote all that facilitates corporate profits at the expense of all else including the wellbeing of the population as a whole.[xxiv] (Image: Benito Mussolini)

In a confidential memo[xxv] (October 16, 2005) to its wealthy clients, the largest bank in the world, Citigroup, informed them of a concept Citigroup called "Plutonomy." This memo provides insight into the thinking of the wealthy of society and their understanding about how they have and will continue to accumulate wealth while the rest of the population remains poor and gets poorer. It is an analysis of the imbalances between the rich and the poor and how to take advantage of the situation and become wealthier. In the memo Citigroup informed them that:

> "The World is dividing into two blocs - the Plutonomy and the rest. The U.S., UK, and Canada are the key Plutonomies - economies powered by the wealthy… the top 1% of households in the U.S., (about 1 million households) accounted for about 20% of overall U.S. income in 2000, slightly smaller than the share of income of the bottom 60% of households put together...In plutonomies the rich absorb a disproportionate chunk of the economy and have a massive impact on reported aggregate numbers like savings rates, current account deficits, consumption levels, etc. the U.S., the top 1% of households also account for 33% of net worth, greater than the bottom 90% of households put together. It gets better (or worse, depending on your political stripe) - the top 1% of households account for 40% of financial net worth, more than the bottom 95% of households put together."
> "Was the U.S. always a plutonomy - powered by the wealthy, who aggrandized larger chunks of the economy to themselves? Not really. For those interested in the details, we recommend "Wealth and Democracy: A Political History of the American Rich" by Kevin Phillips, Broadway Books, 2002."

The charts below illustrate the imbalances in the economy in plutonomy countries versus countries with an egalitarian economic system. [xxvi]

Figure 4. Plutonomy At Work: The Income Share of the Top 1% Has Risen Dramatically Since the Late 1970s in the U.S., the U.K., and Canada

Please see references 18, 4, 22 in the bibliography at the end of the report for the data underlying the chart. Estimates based on tax return data.
Source: Citigroup Investment Research

Figure 5. Of Egalitarian Bent: The Income Share of the Top 1% Is Much Smaller and Is Not Rising as Much, If at All, in Switzerland, the Netherlands, Japan, and France

Please see references 7,17,15,4 in the bibliography at the end of the report for the data underlying the chart. Estimates based on tax return data.
Source: Citigroup Investment Research

The memo goes on to explain that: "At the heart of plutonomy, is income inequality. Societies that are willing to tolerate/endorse income inequality are willing to tolerate/endorse plutonomy." "Organized societies have two ways of expropriating wealth - through the revocation of property rights or through the tax system." Beginning with the Reagan Administration and continued with the Clinton and Bush Administrations, government began to lower taxes for the rich and raise taxes for the other classes of society while colluding with corporations to hold wages down by not increasing the minimum wage and conspiring to allow outsourcing (exporting jobs to countries with cheaper labor) and insourcing (bringing in workers from other countries who will work for less wages) to maintain wages low. Further, the memo does not expect a precipitous drop in the US Dollar but a gradual fall in the dollar and a revaluation of the Chinese currency. Additionally, Citigroup also said that this trend is likely to continue but could be jeopardized by:

> Concentration of wealth and spending in the hands of a few, probably has its limits. What might cause the elastic to snap back? We can see a number of potential challenges to plutonomy. The first, and probably most potent, is through a labor backlash. Outsourcing, offshoring or insourcing of cheap labor is done to undercut current labor costs... Low-end developed market labor might not have much economic power, but it does have equal voting power with the rich...
> A *second* related threat, might come from productive labor no longer maintaining its productive edge...
> A *third* threat comes from the potential social backlash. To use Rawls-ian analysis, the invisible

hand stops working. Perhaps one reason that societies allow plutonomy, is because enough of the electorate believe they have a chance of becoming a Plutoparticipant. Why kill it off, if you can join it? In a sense this is the embodiment of the American dream". But if voters feel they cannot participate, they are more likely to divide up the wealth pie, rather than aspire to being truly rich. Could the plutonomies die because the dream is dead, because enough of society does not believe they can participate? The answer is of course yes. But we suspect this is a threat more clearly felt during recessions, and periods of falling wealth, than when average citizens feel that they are better off.

President Reagan and the moneyed interests he brought with him, epitomized by Donald Regan, as Secretary of The Treasury

Previous to the Reagan years, there was more balance between the incomes of the rich and the rest of the population in the USA economy. President Reagan and the moneyed interests he brought with him, epitomized by Donald Regan, as Secretary of The Treasury, and former CEO of Merrill Lynch (the Goldman Sacks of that day), changed laws to favor the wealthy. Figure #4[xxvii] above demonstrates that the wealthy are susceptible to deflation (a problem that a Citigroup analyst referred to in a subsequent memo as "a policy error leading to asset deflation) since

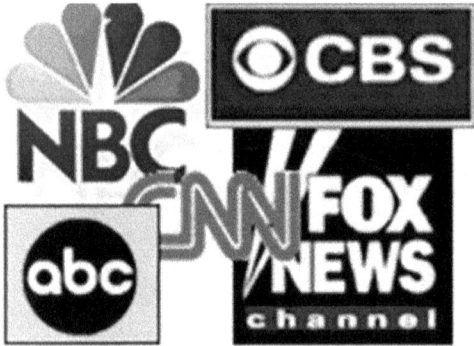

that will reduce their net worth. The wealthy of the USA lost much during the bursting of the "Dot.Com" bubble and the recession between 1999-2002.

Understandably, they would be very keen on promoting economic policies that might re-inflate the bubbles so that the wealthy may regain a portion or all of their lost wealth; this issue is not seen as a serious problem due to the fact that government is sympathetic to policies that favor the wealthy. Nevertheless, prior to 2008 the wealthy, as related in the memo, were really only afraid of one factor, that discontent with plutonomy might reach a level causing the general population to revolt and use their voting rights (the wealthy constitute 1% of the population while the masses constitute 99%) to reverse the economic imbalances by changing tax codes, property rights and the wage structure between labor and capital. This is why it is so important for the wealthy to control the media and government (the lawmaking process), hence the relentless movement towards corporate media consolidation,[xxviii] the glamorizing of the powerful, rich and famous and the perennial presentation of liberals, leftists and socialists as evil traitors as well as deference to corporate and government leaders who are more often portrayed as keepers of the country's trust or as heroes, respectively. There is ever increasing legalized bribery to government officials (campaign contributions to presidents, congress and the judiciary) and support for the military and police forces (to maintain the status quo) as well as the support of the ideal of the USA as a militarily righteous, strong and wrathful country, ready to avenge any indignation coming from other countries. However, any indication that the USA has perpetrated any wrong against other countries is excused away or those who broach the subject tare usually labeled as apologists or wimps. The idea is that people should always remain supportive of the government since it is the supposedly "greatest system ever devised" and has many enemies that are against the "American way of life"; never mind that the USA through it's military or covert operatives (C.I.A.) have interfered with or brought down foreign governments or subjugated the peoples of other countries against their will.[xxix] The media message in general is that USA 'Democracy" and its "Capitalist economic system" are the best systems in human history and should be preserved and protected no matter what inconsistencies or malfeasance may be experienced. The people should always remain convinced that plutonomy is beneficial and should remain as the prevailing system of economics; of course the ideal of plutonomy is not expressed as such but is couched in the ideals of "Democracy", "Capitalism," and "Free Markets." Clearly there is no "Democracy", "Capitalism," and "Free Markets" in operation but rather, plutonomy is what is in operation, in the guise of the USA government, economy and social order; this state of affairs has been in operation for decades. The memo postulates that ordinary people, the masses in the middle class and the poor, tolerate the imbalances caused by plutonomy because of their own greed, that they themselves hope to be one of those wealthy people someday, one of the people who live in luxury by exploiting the rest. That being the case, plutonomy would be self-sustaining and supported by the ignorant masses who aspire to be one of the wealthy and do not understand that it is impossible for all of them to become part of the plutonomy since a plutonomy is predicated upon there being a wealth imbalance in society whereby most of the wealth is possessed or controlled by a small minority (1%); this means that only 1 out of every 100 can become fabulously rich. Furthermore, plutonomy is a foundation for imperialism in that it creates a government that manipulates public opinion, sustains a military industrial complex and the oppression of other nations so that it will retain the favorable economic conditions while making sure that the peoples of other countries do not have the capacity to compete or gain a fair share for their resources. Plutonomy may also be thought of as a form of domestic neo-colonialism (internal imperialism), whereby the elite of the society employ lower echelon members of society to maintain the scheme of the social order. They are to control the rest of the population; in other words, it is a system in which the top 1% control the social, economic and political order through a moderately well to do upper middle class leadership composed of the president, congress, judges, CEO's, military, and police, that imposes the laws and regulations on the rest of the population through a middle class (those who are able to make a living wage and support their families (lower echelon officials (lawyers, police, state legislators, etc.)). Therefore, it might be expected that if there is sufficient unrest in the society, that the wealthy would allow some concessions to labor so as to preserve the present political and economic order: Plutonomy. Presumably, after such concessions, the same plutonomy system would eventually lead to imbalances again in the future. However, if the imbalances should become too great and the elastic of plutonomy should break, there could be widespread social unrest.

In a subsequent internal memo (March 5, 2006)[xxx] Citigroup acknowledges that globalization favors the wealthy and that the wealth imbalance can lead to a backlash.

> Our whole plutonomy thesis is based on the idea that the rich will keep getting richer. This thesis is not without its risks. For example, a policy error leading to asset deflation, would likely damage plutonomy.[xxxi] Furthermore, the rising wealth gap between the rich and poor will probably at some point lead to a political backlash. Whilst the rich are getting a greater share of the wealth, and the poor a lesser share, political enfranchisement remains as one person, one vote (in the plutonomies). At some point it is likely that labor will fight back against the rising profit share of the rich and there will be a political backlash against the rising wealth of the rich. This could be felt

through higher taxation (on the rich or indirectly though higher corporate taxes/regulation) or through trying to protect indigenous laborers, in a push-back on globalization either anti-immigration, or protectionism. We don t see this happening yet, though there are signs of rising political tensions. However we are keeping a close eye on developments.

citigroup

See page 33 for Analyst Certification and Important Disclosures

Industry Note

Equity Strategy

Plutonomy: Buying Luxury, Explaining Global Imbalances

October 16, 2005

Ajay Kapur, CFA
+1-212-816-4813
ajay.kapur@citigroup.com

Niall Macleod
+44-20-7986-4449
niall.j.macleod@citigroup.com

Narendra Singh
+1-212-816-2807
narendra.singh@citigroup.com

SUMMARY

> The World is dividing into two blocs - the Plutonomy and the rest. The U.S., UK, and Canada are the key Plutonomies - economies powered by the wealthy. Continental Europe (ex-Italy) and Japan are in the egalitarian bloc.

> Equity risk premium embedded in "global imbalances" are unwarranted. In plutonomies the rich absorb a disproportionate chunk of the economy and have a massive impact on reported aggregate numbers like savings rates, current account deficits, consumption levels, etc. This imbalance in inequality expresses itself in the standard scary " global imbalances". We worry less.

> There is no "average consumer" in a Plutonomy. Consensus analyses focusing on the "average" consumer are flawed from the start. The Plutonomy Stock Basket outperformed MSCI AC World by 6.8% per year since 1985. Does even better if equities beat housing. Select names: Julius Baer, Bulgari, Richemont, Kuoni, and Toll Brothers.

Global

| WELCOME TO THE PLUTONOMY MACHINE

In early September we wrote about the (ir)relevance of oil to equities and introduced the idea that the U.S. is a Plutonomy - a concept that generated great interest from our clients. As global strategists, this got us thinking about how to buy stocks based on this plutonomy thesis, and the subsequent thesis that it will gather strength and amass breadth. In researching this idea on a global level and looking for stock ideas we also chanced upon some interesting big picture implications. This process manifested itself

What did Citigroup have to say about the current economic situation?

Citigroup says gold could rise above $2,000 next year as world unravels

Gold is poised for a dramatic surge and could blast through $2,000 an ounce by the end of next year as central banks flood the world's monetary system with liquidity, according to an internal client note from the US bank Citigroup.

By Ambrose Evans-Pritchard Published: 4:33PM
GMT 26 Nov 2008[xxxii]

In a more recent memo now taking into account the crash of the economy in the Fall of 2009, Tom Fitzpatrick, Citibank's chief technical strategist states:

> "The world is not going back to normal after the magnitude of what they have done. When the dust settles this will either work, and the money they have pushed into the system will feed through into an inflation shock..."

He goes on to explain that the massive money creation efforts by the Federal Reserve and other central banks will end with one of two things: A resurgence of inflation, or a fall into "depression, civil disorder and possibly wars." Additionally, the memo states that gold will rise to over $2,000 per ounce, and that these events will come to pass either in 2009 or 2010.

Telegraph.co.uk

Home News Sport Finance Lifestyle Comment Travel Culture Technology Fashion Jobs Dating Games Offers

News by Sector Comment Personal Finance Markets Economics Your Business Alex iPhone App Finance Blogs Fund Game

Ambrose Evans-Pritchard Jeff Randall Damian Reece Edmund Conway Tracy Corrigan Jeremy Warner Liam Halligan

HOME › FINANCE › COMMENT › AMBROSE EVANS-PRITCHARD

Citigroup says gold could rise above $2,000 next year as world unravels

Gold is poised for a dramatic surge and could blast through $2,000 an ounce by the end of next year as central banks flood the world's monetary system with liquidity, according to an internal client note from the US bank Citigroup.

By Ambrose Evans-Pritchard
Published: 4:18PM GMT 26 Nov 2008

An employee at Tanaka Kikinzoku Jewelry K.K. displays a gold bar at the company's store in Tokyo. Photo: Reuters

The bank said the damage caused by the financial excesses of the last quarter century was forcing the world's authorities to take steps that had never been tried before.

This gamble was likely to end in one of two extreme ways, with either a resurgence of inflation or a downward spiral into depression, civil disorder, and

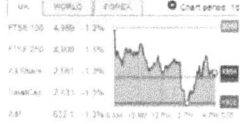

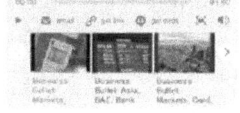

GIVEN THE AFORESAID, WHAT CAN WE EXPECT IN THE NEAR AND INTERMEDIATE TERM?

1.   Further bursting of the residential real estate bubble will continue –this means that the equity that was in real estate has or will continue to vanish – this means even less people spending illusory moneys from illusory home equity wealth that was sustaining the bubble economy – and also means more economic depression will develop. Economies can appear to do well for certain periods of time even while they are in a downward spiral. KEEP IN MIND—the crash that started the Great Depression of the 1930's was an initial 48% decline in the stock market which was followed by a 50% recovery (of the 48% loss) – just as we have seen today. Yet in the 1930s the economy then fell (after the

supposed recovery) again until it lost 90% of its value and real estate also lost equal value – (this is called the "bottom"). So a house that was worth $100,000 in 1929 was worth $10,000 by 1932. (this is what can happen due to economic depression and *Deflation*). It took 3 years for the US economy to get to the bottom while there were intermittent market rallies wherein it appeared that the economy was recovering and government leaders as well as business leaders were claiming that the depression was over –as they are today. Japan experienced a deflationary depression during it's "Lost Decade" of the 1990's (such a scenario is possible for the USA). Stocks in Japan enjoyed *FIVE* different bear market rallies — *averaging +50%* — over the past two decades, yet stocks sank to new lows each time. And today, Japan's Nikkei is still down about -70% from its former peak (in 1989). So it never has recovered. I am not arguing that the U.S. will follow the Japan model, but it is a possibility; but that would be a best case scenario if it were possible. There are some big differences that point to a more dire scenario for the outcome of the crisis of the USA – Japan did not have the MASSIVE debt that the USA has and the Japanese people, the consumers, had cash and savings before and after the downturn unlike the majority of the population in the USA which is saddled with personal debt (mortgages, credit cards, etc.). So the US collapse would be much harder and would last longer since less members of the population have money to spend to "get the economy going". The depression of the 1930's was a "DEFLATIONARY DEPRESSION". Back in the 1930's the government did not apply *quantitative easing-* or *liquidity* theories[xxxiii] in an effort to stave off deflation. The government officials and Wall Street financiers are trying to avoid a Deflation by printing lots of money (what they call euphemistically *quantitative easing-* or *liquidity*) and that will lead to the collapse of the dollar and the economy through excessive inflation. They feel that inflation is better and easier to control than deflation. This is not supported by the history of other countries that had their currencies blow up (like Argentina, Zimbabwe, and others). Due to the massive National Debt and the massive bailouts and war spending and other malfeasance we are more likely to have an "INFLATIONARY DEPRESSION"[xxxiv] (depression of asset values (like homes) and depression of economic activity and at the same time massive rise in interest rates and cost of goods). An inflationary depression would be like the inflation of the late 1970's[xxxv] in the USA but much worse – devastating the economy.

Top Searches
1. Stock Picking
2. Forex
3. Options Trading
4. Credit Crisis

Dictionary

Articles

Investing Basics
Stocks
Mutual Funds
FOREX
ETFs
Active Trading
Bonds

Hot Penny Stock Picks

Home > Articles

The Great Inflation Of The 1970s

by Gregory Bresiger (Contact Author | Biography)

Email Article   Print   Feedback   Reprints   BOOKMARK

It's the 1970s, and the stock market is a mess. It loses 40% in an 18-month period, and for close to a decade few people want anything to do with stocks. Economic growth is weak, which results in rising unemployment that eventually reaches double-digits. The easy-money policies of the American central bank, which were designed to generate full employment, by the early 1970s, also caused high inflation. The central bank, under different leadership, would later reverse its policies, raising interest rates to some 20%, a number once considered usurious. For interest-sensitive industries, such as housing and cars, rising interest rates cause a calamity. With interest rates skyrocketing, many people are priced out of new cars and homes. (Learn more in A Review Of Past Recessions.)

2. Now also the bursting of the commercial real estate bubble----have you noticed more vacancies in malls and shopping centers? Wait for the ghost malls next! –this means businesses closing, bankruptcies, less economic activity and more unemployment because less small businesses are able to operate and more depression will be generated.

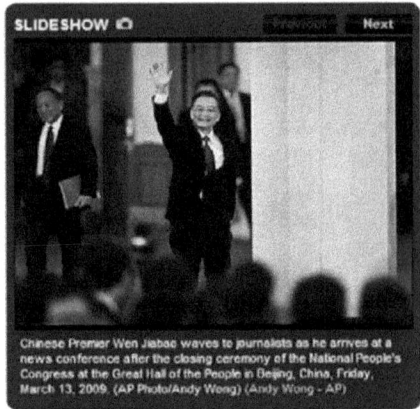

The Washington Post TODAY'S NEWSPAPER
Subscribe | PostPoints

NEWS | POLITICS | OPINIONS | BUSINESS | LOCAL | SPORTS | ARTS & LIVING | GOING OUT GUIDE

SEARCH: [go] • washingtonpost.com ◯ Web : Results by Google | Se

washingtonpost.com > World > Asia/Pacific

Find the World Desk on: ◼ Facebook ◯ Twitter ◼ Friendfeed ◻ Your Phone

China Worried About U.S. Debt
Biggest Creditor Nation Demands A Guarantee

By Anthony Faiola
Washington Post Staff Writer
Saturday, March 14, 2009; Page A01

SLIDESHOW ◻   Previous | Next

Exerting its new influence as the U.S. government's largest creditor, China yesterday demanded that the Obama administration "guarantee the safety" of its $1 trillion in American bonds as Washington goes further into debt to combat the economic crisis.

Chinese Premier Wen Jinbao made the demand at the end of the National People's Congress in Beijing at a time when relations between the two nations show fresh signs of strain.

Chinese Premier Wen Jiabao waves to journalists as he arrives at a news conference after the closing ceremony of the National People's Congress at the Great Hall of the People in Beijing, China, Friday, March 13, 2009. (AP Photo/Andy Wong) (Andy Wong - AP)

"We have lent a huge amount of money to the U.S. Of course we are concerned about the safety of our assets," Wen said. "To be honest, I am

TOOLBOX
◻ Resize 📄 Print ✉ E-mail

3. The dollar will continue to decline every year until it is worthless – like what happened to the currencies in Argentina, Mexico, Ecuador and other places. The dollar has lost most of its value since 1971 when the USA went off the partial gold standard backing the US Dollar. Now the US Dollar has lost almost all its value since 1913 –it is worth

only $0.03 (3 cents) of the original dollar of 1913 (the dollar of the year 2009 buys only 3 cents of what the 1913 dollar could buy) due to the creation of the Federal Reserve which prints money based on nothing – just making money out of thin air with the intent of intentionally creating inflation (the more money printed the less value each previous dollar has), and deficit government spending. This means that the savings and wealth of anyone who owns dollars will be eventually completely lost. But those who have access to the money first (banks, Federal Reserve, etc.), as it is printed, and are able to purchase assets, will retain their wealth and will see it increase through inflation (given, of course, that there is no "policy error leading to asset deflation"). The US National Debt and what has been taken on for bailouts along with the mishandling of Social Security and Medicare funds has led to a situation where the debts owed by the US Government can never be paid. The national debt of the USA is now $11.9 trillion and the GDP of the USA is now $10.5 trillion[xxxvi] ---so the USA now produces less than the amount of the National debt before all of the expenses of the government and the interest payment on the debt ---this is a deficit and any more borrowing or spending is deficit spending. There is no surplus to pay for the debt itself. The economic state of the USA government is "bankruptcy." (**bankruptcy** -The financial status of a firm that has been legally judged either to have debts that exceed assets or to be unable to pay its bills.)[xxxvii] The moneys that were borrowed to create the economic bubbles went to people who used the moneys to buy vacations, SUVs, boats, cars, big screen TVs, luxury items, etc. and did not go into building factories or other manufacturing or industrial infrastructure investments that could be now used for income producing purposes which would produce sufficient income to pay for the national debt through higher paying jobs and taxes. The solution that has been adopted is to create more money, and allow it to be devalued so that the debt can be paid with devalued dollars. The side effect of this strategy is high inflation, which eats away at the value of the currency. The Chinese, who are the largest holders of US Government Debt, have expressed displeasure[xxxviii] at this strategy (*quantitative easing* – (printing dollars to devalue the currency and to produce inflation)) and have set about to dispose of as much debt they can without pushing the US Dollar into an out of control downward spiral, destroying the value of their dollar holdings as well. Governments around the world that have been buying US Debt (Treasury Bonds-that have allowed the US Government to finance its National Debt) have begun to stop doing that and this development will eventually stop sustaining the false (bubble) US economy. As of Sep. 2009, *China is now a net SELLER of U.S. Treasury notes and bonds!* (http://www.moneyandmarkets.com) (They are selling more than they buy). This is why the Federal Reserve (US Central Bank) has been buying the US Government debt, to make up for what they are not selling to prospective buyers. (Would it not be nice if you could spend all your money and money you borrowed and then make yourself a loan by just printing more money for yourself? How long can this go on? How long will people accept your bogus money based on no wealth or assets –because in reality you are bankrupt? As long as people need to sustain you so they do not lose the money they lent you?) It is interesting that unlike the past when everyone believed in the US Dollar, now many people do not want to be paid in US Dollars any more. They are, whenever possible, avoiding income streams (wages, fees, commissions, etc.) denominated in US Dollars. Consider a representative case:

"Supermodel 'rejects dollar pay' The world's richest model has reportedly reacted in her own way to the sliding value of the US dollar - by refusing to be paid in the currency. Gisele Bündchen is said to be keen to avoid the US currency because of uncertainty over its strength.* (6 November 2007)
http://news.bbc.co.uk/2/hi/7078612.stm

4. We are beyond the tipping point of US debt and further collapse may be triggered next month or a year from now --by any number of social, political

and or economic factors but for now everyone in the financial community and government is trying to sustain things –saying anything positive and nothing negative–hoping the economy will improve enough to pay for the debt and bailouts - but the fundamentals of the economy do not support such an expectation. In order to pay debts it is necessary to have sufficient income to live on and additional to pay down the debts. For a country, the additional income, the surpluses are supposed to come from manufacturing, the production of valuable items that other countries may want. If that is not possible then a trade imbalance occurs which leads to trade deficits. Since the USA gave up it's manufacturing base for the sake of short term higher profits through outsourcing, there is no large scale manufacturing base to draw upon; and there are no other large scale innovative industries emerging to take its place. Whether a crash (fast decline) or a slow decline occurs, a decline is probable. The debt, wars, past and present bailouts, aging population, Medicare and Medicaid commitments, etc. mean economic recovery is impossible without substantial devaluation of assets and loss of income and loss of living standards (the USA will be a second world economy and places like China and India and Europe will take its place). The USA population will be poor and there is a possibility of social unrest (riots, violence, etc.) as occurred recently in Iceland. The people in Iceland brought down the government due to displeasure over the collapse of the economy and the currency ---think about it --- Iceland is a "civilized country" – are people in the USA "civilized"?---will the powers that be in the USA allow "the people" to "take down the government"?---what would they do in response and what chaos could ensue?) Many people in the USA draw comfort from their guns and other weapons that the second amendment to the constitution allows. Those who feel that way have not realized that the government wields greater force. Citizens would not be capable of resisting unpopular government actions and ultimately resistors would suffer a similar fate as any unarmed population, a massacre. Considering the treatment of protestors at recent political conventions (strong-arm tactics to keep them at bay and to minimize their protests, brutalizing (police violence), falsely accusing protestors (as well as bystanders and journalists[xxxix]) of misconduct to arrest them on false charges,[xl] etc.) it may be extrapolated that a more serious challenge to authority would be met with greater violence, mass detentions and possible breakdown of law and order altogether, up to and including martial law as well as suspension of the constitution (which would, at that point be a mere formality).

There are presently TWO major dangers ahead:

1. **ANOTHER CRASH LIKE FALL 2008.** The crash was a deflationary crash due to the realization of the true condition of the US economy and the loss of credit because those with money realized that banks were filled with toxic assets and the overleveraged consumer could not support the subprime mortgage debt (causing massive losses to banking and the real estate industries that rippled throughout the economy). The situation has not improved but rather is just being held together with illusory bailouts and stimulus programs and financial markets are "hoping" the economic activity will improve enough to absorb the losses. That is not possible do to the massive debt and even more massive amount of toxic securities that were created. The average consumer – who makes up 70% of the US economy through spending, has pulled back due to loss of jobs, high cost of health insurance and unemployment. Again, since the USA gave up its manufacturing base due to the dubious ideal of outsourcing to countries with cheaper labor costs so that corporations could make more profits there is little manufacturing capacity to create items

of wealth that people around the world would want to buy ---thus bringing wealth into the USA. So there is real danger of another crash- and further collapse of the economy until its valuation reaches the true value of its assets.

  a. which would mean more devaluation of assets (like the reduction of real estate values) which would lead to more loss of wealth and more depression of economic activity, more job losses and business failures, bankruptcies, etc.

  b. In fact, as the US Dollar becomes devalued, any assets valued in US Dollars could suffer devaluation.

2. **COLLAPSE OF THE US DOLLAR**. Currently, the US dollar has been collapsing slowly (has lost 60% of

its value versus the Euro and Gold just since the year 2000. This will continue and will mean that things will continue to get more expensive – though people who have Euros or other currencies will find things priced in US Dollars cheap. For holders of US Dollars, services will be cheaper but items to purchase, even from China, will be expensive. So everyone except the wealthy will see loss in their standard of living. Consequently, the US Dollar is doomed to fail and will eventually lose world currency reserve status. This may happen fast or slow. Many countries have begun to lay the foundation for a move away from the US Dollar as the world's reserve currency.[xli]

    a. If there is a sudden devaluation of the US Dollar you could wake up one day and read in the news that the US Dollar is not worth half of what it was worth yesterday – can be done by government decree – has happened before.

    b. It can happen slow as it has been happening over a number of years – the price of Euros and Gold and foreign stocks, real estate and other property and anything else the dollar

could buy in the USA will cost more but
foreign items will rise much much more in
reference to the US dollar

ONE MORE FACTOR: one more factor on top of all this is the retirement in mass of "Baby Boomers"–people born between 1945-1962. This means that the foundation of the consumer economy will start to shift from those having more people contributing to the economy to more people dependent on the economy. This demographic factor (more drag on the economy) also means economic slowdown and recession –and on top of everything else (the economic crash due to malfeasance (mishandling of the Social Security and Medicare/Medicaid funds), dollar collapse) will keep the US economy down for years.[xlii]

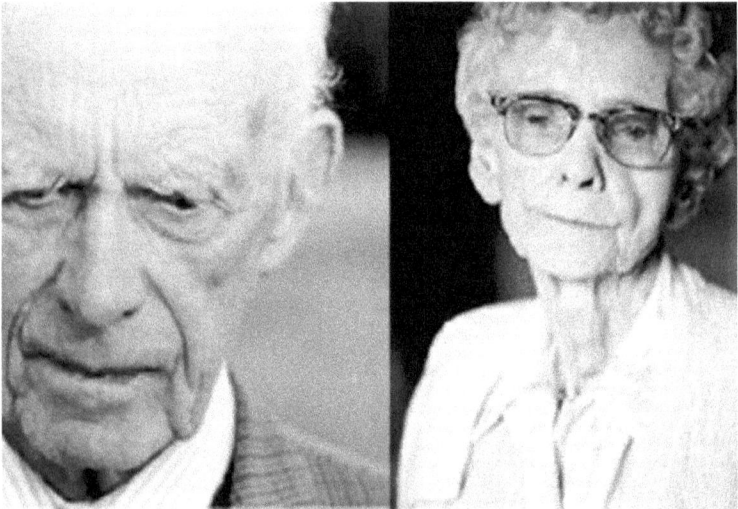

WHAT TO DO ABOUT THE **TWO** MAIN DANGERS RIGHT NOW?

1. In case of another ECONOMIC CRASH (sharp decline in stocks and real estate and other assets):

a. To protect from an economic deflationary crash

   i. Get out of debts that do not allow you to save and invest for the future- economic conditions that may be severe.

   ii. get out of real estate (do not be tempted by currently falling real estate prices) and any major assets based on US Dollar denominations and go to cash.

   iii. put the cash in foreign currencies and wait for the full economic collapse and then afterwards buy assets with the higher valued foreign currencies when the dollar is further devalued.

   1. place the moneys to work in safe investments based in foreign currencies. See an advisor for your particular situation.

   iv. If you are treading water financially due to high real estate costs -One strategy- get out of high cost house and live in lower cost rental. Find a decent location with lower real estate values. Find a smaller property. Do not worry about credit rating since getting caught up in the financial collapse without savings is worse than having bad credit (which can be cleaned up within 3-5 years.)

v. Do not take on new debts or create family situations (like having more children for the next few years) that will drain resources and prevent savings.

vi. Reduce expenses- live in cheaper house, drive cheaper car, less extravagant living, etc. so you can save and invest for the future.

vii. If you are currently in school or college or undergoing job training make sure you are studying a subject that will be in demand when you graduate; otherwise you may find that the new depressed economy has no place for your expertise. Gain training in occupations that will be needed regardless of the economic conditions and if possible occupations that are in demand around the world so that you can be mobile if you need to be.

viii. Another strategy

1. If you can live safely and comfortably consider living in areas that are less populated and where it is easier to live a self sustained life with lower expenses (lower utility costs, less dependency on foreign products, processed foods, and higher taxes).

2. If you can relocate to another country consider living in a country where funds will be worth more.

a. You can live in a country where the dollar is still worth more than the local currency. (Ex. Bermuda, East Timor, Ecuador, El Salvador, Federated States of Micronesia, Marshall Islands, Palau, Panama, Turks and Caicos Islands.)

b. If you place funds in currencies other than the dollar, and live in a country that uses the US Dollar (including the USA-but USA may be undesirable due to social unrest especially in big cities) the expenses will be cheaper to live in as far as services and other expenses.

b. Get out of the stock market as an investor– do not invest or "buy and hold" stocks. The stock market can have another crash at any time and should only be approached for short term trading and not following the Wall Street media or anything said by government officials or Wall Street executives. Experienced people can make trading investments that will go up as the stock market goes down.

c. Avoid Bond Funds

d. Avoid adjustable rate debt – (when interest rates go up – watch out) eventually the Federal Reserve will be forced to raise interest rates from an artificially low, near 0% now- to save the dollar. There is no choice but this will devastate the economy anyway because there is no strength to withstand it – people have little wealth and little income.

e. Do not depend on pensions – you see what happened to pension funds and 401Ks and IRAs in 2008 (loss of 50% or more of value). Take control of your finances and make your retirement program free from toxic economies and bogus financial investments. If you can, change your investments from US Dollar denominated securities and assets to a foreign securities, gold and silver foundation.

f. The government could conceivably confiscate pension funds in order to pay down the USA Government debt.

2. In case of CURRENCY CRISIS (sharp decline in US Dollar)

a. To protect from a dollar collapse change moneys from dollars to foreign currencies, gold and silver

b. US Dollar denominated CDs and T-Bills are not safe because if there were continued devaluation of the US Dollar you WILL get your money back but what will it be worth when you get it back? http://www.americasbubbleeconomy.com/ABEspecialRepo rt100306.pdf

c. Of course you should maintain a proper amount needed to take care of day to day and monthly expenses but your disposable funds should be placed in a safe place.

OTHER STRATEGIES

1. Some of the ideas raised in this paper for saving wealth may require a certain amount of funds or you may not think you can do this alone. If you think you do not have enough funds you should pool your resources with others of like mind. Join others of like mind to discuss and educate yourself about the issues raised in this paper. Then develop a plan of action that can be successful with your pooled resources strategies.

2. If you have the capacity to live in a decent area in a sustainable fashion and you are able to afford your lifestyle while saving and implementing a foreign currency strategy you may remain in the USA. There may be short term opportunities to engage in commerce, work in your profession etc. However, the social/political/economic conditions may deteriorate at any time.

3. If possible be prepared to leave the country until the economic unrest has settled.

d. At that time real estate will be cheap

e. Crime will be under control

f. There will be a possibility to rebuild the economy and there will be economic opportunities then

   i. This outlook cannot occur before 2013 at the earliest.

4. For those who do not have the capacity to leave and or have no need to conserve substantial assets:

a. Make alliances with neighbors for security and cooperation

b. Accumulate consumable items like toiletries, dried foods and other items that will go up when the crises become progressively worse.

c. If you have any spare funds, whenever you have spare funds, even if it is only $10 or $20 at a time, per week, per month or every 2 or 3 months, purchase "junk silver", silver rounds and store them in a safe place. This will rise in value and it can also be used as currency in a worse case scenario. You can purchase these at a coin dealer or online – (see resources section below.). You take possession of the silver.

d. The idea above can also be applied with a stock broker acc at a firm like Scottrade, Think or Swim, E-Trade, etc. But here you do not take possession of the silver. You can purchase the silver Exchange Traded Fund (ETF) called "SLV". The benefit is that you do not need to store it but in the event of an emergency it would take a few days to cash in. So you may consider a combination of both strategies if you are able to save over $500-$1000.

5. If it is not possible to leave the country prepare to live with less wealth; communicate and plan with others about how to provide for safety, food and other necessities in case of emergency.

g. If you can't leave the country at least let your money leave the country. Then you can live well in a devalued economy with foreign money to buy devalued items based on the devalued US Dollar. Open a foreign currency acc inside the country (there are 1-2 banks that do this) but realize the banks inside the country can have their assets confiscated (has happened before). Or do it outside in places like Panama, Cayman Islands, Denmark, etc.

Appendix 1

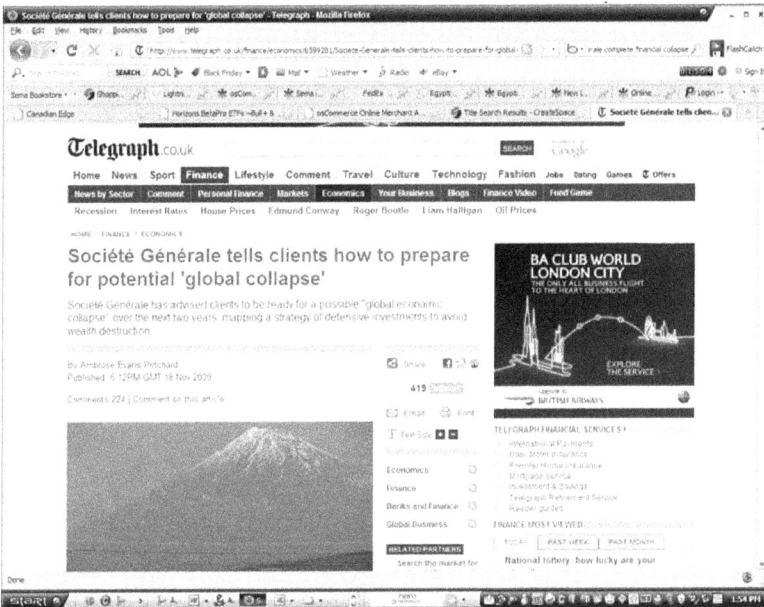

Société Générale tells clients how to prepare for potential 'global collapse'
Société Générale has advised clients to be ready for a possible "global economic collapse" over the next two years, mapping a strategy of defensive investments to avoid wealth destruction.[4]

By Ambrose Evans-Pritchard
Published: 6:12PM GMT 18 Nov 2009
Explosion of debt: Japan's public debt could reach as much as 270pc of GDP in the next two years. A bullet train is pictured speeding past Mount Fuji in Fuji city, west of Tokyo Photo: Reuters

---

[4] http://www.telegraph.co.uk/finance/economics/6599281/Societe-Generale-tells-clients-how-to-prepare-for-global-collapse.html

In a report entitled "Worst-case debt scenario", the bank's asset team said state rescue packages over the last year have merely transferred private liabilities onto sagging sovereign shoulders, creating a fresh set of problems. Overall **debt is still far too high in almost all rich economies** as a share of GDP (350pc in the US), whether public or private. It must be reduced by the hard slog of "deleveraging", for years.

Appendix 2

'Debt levels risk another crisis[5]

"As yet, nobody can say with any certainty whether we have in fact escaped the prospect of a global economic collapse," said the 68-page report, headed by asset chief Daniel Fermon. It is an exploration of the dangers, not a forecast.

Under the French bank's "Bear Case" scenario (the gloomiest of three possible outcomes), the dollar would slide further and global equities would retest the March (2009) lows. Property prices would tumble again. Oil would fall back to $50 in 2010.

Governments have already shot their fiscal bolts. Even without fresh spending, public debt would explode within two years to 105pc of GDP in the UK, 125pc in the US and the eurozone, and 270pc in Japan. Worldwide state debt would reach $45 trillion, up two-and-a-half times in a decade.

(UK figures look low because debt started from a low base. Mr. Ferman said the UK would converge with Europe at 130pc of GDP by 2015 under the bear case).

The underlying debt burden is greater than it was after the Second World War, when nominal levels looked similar. Ageing populations will make it harder to erode debt through growth. "High public debt looks entirely unsustainable in the long run. We have almost reached a point of no return for government debt," it said.

---

[5] http://www.telegraph.co.uk/finance/financetopics/g20-summit/6228450/Debt-levels-risk-another-crisis.html

Inflating debt away might be seen by some governments as a lesser of evils.

If so, gold would go "up, and up, and up" as the only safe haven from fiat paper money. Private debt is also crippling. Even if the US savings rate stabilizes at 7pc, and all of it is used to pay down debt, it will still take nine years for households to reduce debt/income ratios to the safe levels of the 1980s.

The bank said the current crisis displays "compelling similarities" with Japan during its Lost Decade (or two), with a big difference: Japan was able to stay afloat by exporting into a robust global economy and by letting the yen fall. It is not possible for half the world to pursue this strategy at the same time.

SocGen advises bears to sell the dollar and to "short" cyclical equities such as technology, auto, and travel to avoid being caught in the "inherent deflationary spiral". Emerging markets would not be spared. Paradoxically, they are more leveraged to the US growth than Wall Street itself. Farm commodities would hold up well, led by sugar.

Mr. Fermon said junk bonds would lose 31pc of their value in 2010 alone. However, sovereign bonds would "generate turbo-charged returns" mimicking the secular slide in yields seen in Japan as the slump ground on. At one point Japan's 10-year yield dropped to 0.40pc. The Fed would hold down yields by purchasing more bonds. The European Central Bank would do less, for political reasons.

SocGen's case for buying sovereign bonds is controversial. A number of funds doubt whether the Japan scenario will be repeated, not least because Tokyo itself may be on the cusp of a debt compound crisis.

Mr. Fermon said his report had electrified clients on both sides of the Atlantic. "Everybody wants to know what the impact will be. A lot of hedge funds and bankers are worried," he said.

Appendix 3

Nov. 3, 2010 Update

As of Early November 2010 the foreclosure problem of the United States of America continued to worsen. Unemployment remained high as the 2009 Stimulus Bill which pumped over $700 Billion into the economy, passed by President Obama and the congress, expired. Banks continued to invest in emerging markets, trade on Wall Street and not give loans to individuals or small businesses. While Wall Street did well, as expected the general economy remained stagnant. Through all of this the Democratic party sought to pass legislation such as the stimulus, the health care reform and the wall street reform bills that did not go far enough to resolve the underlying problem with the economy, malfeasance due to greed in which the top 1% of the population have more wealth and income than the rest.

The Republican Party remained obstructive, trying to hold up any initiatives of the president or the democrats, so they could point to failure and have political gains in the next elections. The passage of the "Citizens United" case, which allows corporations to make unlimited political donations, in the Supreme Court, dominated by corporate favoring justices, where corporations were granted the right to spend unlimited amounts of money advocating for particular parties and candidates served to overwhelm those politicians desiring to bring real and substantial reforms to the government. Amidst all of this the "Tea Party", a movement of conservative, libertarian and regressive social advocates, gained inroads in the elections as republican candidates accepted by the Republican party. The dissatisfaction of Democrats and independent voters with the legislation put out by the democrats coupled with a countermovement of fear and anxiety spurred by right wing television and radio talk show hosts, right wing think tanks, "Fox News" 24/7 broadcasts and the corporate capacity to blanket television and radio shows and advertisements with hate speech, fear speech and demagoguery changed sufficient minds in the electorate to allow the republicans to regain control of the House of Representatives and reduce the Democratic party majority in the Senate.

Some annalists now expect that the same political situation that occurred under the presidency of Bill Clinton will occur again. Then, the republicans regained control and Clinton was no longer solely to blame for the economic conditions. The republicans were no longer able to say no to everything the Democrats proposed and they were forced to deal with Clinton.

There are some differences between now and then however. The Federal Reserve had never tried quantitative easing, which admittedly, is an experiment and they do not know if it will work and prevent depression or if done wrong would lead to hyperinflation and economic collapse anyway. Then there was no powerful right wing 24/7 media and no corporate capacity to blanket the airwaves with hate speech, fear speech and demagoguery with unlimited funds. Further, there was no foreclosure debacle and the government and personal debt was much lower. The social fabric was not as frayed; there was no resurgence of racism towards African Americans and Latinos as there is at present. The political landscape as far as concerns the political parties, has been left in a highly polarized condition where the parties control regions of the country. For example, most southern states are now controlled by the Republicans and most northern states are controlled by the Democratic Party. This condition has now fueled serious speculation as to the long-term viability of the USA as a united country and the possibility of a breakup into states or regions composed of states or at least an ineffective Federal government and powerful states, which could lead to the loss of power as a country and a surge in power of local governments that are more responsive to the racism, xenophobia and sexism of the baser elements and more controllable by the oligarchy or plutocracy.[6] Needless to say, if such changes were to come about there would be large scale social and political upheaval.

Therefore, whether or not the president is able to work with congress to bring forth meaningful legislation (unlikely given the large divide between the ideologies and the incapacity to do what is necessary to fix the economy that would in the short term lead to more unemployment and suffering) the situation will continue since foreclosures are

[6] http://www.lewrockwell.com/rozeff/rozeff328.html,
http://www.youtube.com/watch?v=3yRzQz0KMyI&feature=related

increasing now, not just because of subprime mortgages but because prime mortgages (given to those with good credit and who were employed at that time) are also failing. The real estate market is expected to decline until the year 2012 before beginning a reversal that will take many years.

In the first half of 2010 the US Dollar saw a surge but by the middle of 2010 it began to decline again and gold saw new highs it had not seen since the 1980s. So the situation with the US Dollar remains negative as the Federal Reserve instituted "Quantitative Easing" (creating money out of thin air and injecting money into the economy) to boost prices (cause inflation) and sustain markets. The stimulus and "Quantitative Easing" #1 (*$1.7 trillion*) ran out and towards the second half of 2010 the economy began again to falter. On November 3, 2010 the Federal Reserve announced it would continue with its policies (QE #2). This will undoubtedly lead to a decrease in value of the US Dollar. Nevertheless, at the same time, since the overall economic policies favor continued "Reaganomics" ("trickledown economics," "voodoo economics") tax cuts for the rich, policies allowing corporations to close factories in the USA and using near slave labor in foreign countries, no increase in wages, and no investment in the domestic economy in areas such as education and infrastructure or alternative energy, the economy will continue to be controlled by corporate powers through corrupt politicians. In scope and size this makes the USA economy the most corrupt in history due to its size and negative effect (wealth transfer from rich and middle classes to the rich) on its own population and the world population.

The "Tea Party" conservative movement had been trying to get the government to take a more conservative economic stance. The Republican Party pandered to them in order to gain their support so they could have a majority to control congress. Now that they have won that majority those in the Tea Party will expect them to institute austerity measures, primarily cutting social services. The Tea Party movement is composed of mostly white males and females over 50 years of age, people in or close to retirement who have already lived most of their working productive lives. The cuts now would mostly affect the young as well as those who are part of the middle and lower class as well as the poor. So, if the austerity measures are instituted we may expect a backlash from the poor and the impoverished middle class who form the majority, which would lead to social unrest. Additionally, if such austerity measures were instituted, the middle class and the poor would have less money and the economy would collapse, fall apart and enter into full on depression; investors would sell everything and take their money out of the country to invest in emerging and stable developed economies. If the measures are not instituted we could see the "Tea Party" movement grow to a degree where a viable third party could emerge that would challenge the two party system. Failing to achieve success, the "Tea Party" movement could become the leading edge of those who do not want to be part of the country and see it as a failed experiment, leading to calls for secession. We can expect a conflict between those who want to spend money to stimulate the economy and those who want fiscal conservatism and austerity which in the short term will lead to gridlock while the economy further deteriorates until emergency like conditions force some action to help the situation. Help here can be of two types; help to aid those who are left destitute or help to stimulate the economy which will lead to greater fiscal malfeasance and greater and prolonged downturn later on. Such a gridlock could lead to destabilization as economic distress leads to social distress and social distress leads to political distress.

However, the Federal Reserve is still free to print money to supposedly stimulate the economy but due to the overall economic condition it is unlikely to work and the banks would take that money as they did previously, to invest in world stock markets; rather, this would cause further devaluation of the US Dollar and further decline of the overall economy in the long run. In the short run prices would go up (due to the devaluation of the dollar that would occur because of the new money printing by the Federal Reserve; this also means the money people may still have left buys less, hence their wealth has been reduced by the actions of the Federal Reserve) but since wages have not gone up, people would not be able to afford many things and would reduce spending. Since consumer spending is at least 65% of the economy, this would spur further recession and depression in a cycle of more business closings and bankruptcies since they do not have enough consumers to sustain their businesses.

> From last July 2010 to October 2010, margarine prices have risen 6 percent. Women's dresses are up 6 percent. Beer is up 6 percent. Milk prices have risen 6.5 percent. Candy is 13 percent more expensive. Butter is up 19 percent. Shoes are up a whopping 45 percent.

The pseudo-capitalistic (corporate welfare [subsidizes corporations instead of letting them succeed or fail according to real economic conditions]) form of economics of the USA is susceptible to business cycles of boom and bust since it is not based on real economic activity but rather speculative stock markets and irresponsible government spending or corrupt government spending that favors corporate insiders. The money created by the FED is then available to fuel speculative bubbles and campaign donations to bribe congress to allow more and more straying from sound economics. If the country were based in ethical culture of economics it could be prudent to have government spending (even deficit spending) to maintain jobs and other economic activity during the lean times; then it would pull back (pay back the debt) during the boom years. However, the distortion, malfeasance and corruption has led to a condition of bankruptcy and criminal conspiracy with corporate entities (fascism) which has rendered the federal government incapable of producing fair and sensible legislation, receiving little trust from the populace. The rise in gold signals a loss of confidence in the economy and rise in confidence in items perceived as having real worth (gold, commodities) as opposed to paper money which has no intrinsic value and can be created out of thin air for the purposes and designs of the wealthy in a way that steals the value of the money and the wealth of those who do not have the power to create it (those other than the top 1% of the population). This means that while fiscal conservatism is a more viable form of economics, it is too late to apply strict fiscally conservative regulations on an economy that has surpassed any semblance of fiscal soundness; the foundations of the US economy are defunct due to malfeasance, greed and lust for power. It is gutted, hollow, and bankrupt, sustained only by the US Dollar status as reserve currency and the subsidies from other countries that buy US Bonds. The only solutions to the underlying problem of the malfeasance in the USA economy are to change from a greed basis to a sustainability focus and cut spending drastically and raise taxes or wipe away debt (which would leave creditors with a loss). Since the wealthy who bankrupted the country in the first place, as they enriched themselves, will not allow the wiping away of debt (as would be done in bankruptcy court), the malaise and depressive conditions will continue but also the hold (power to control) of creditors on the economy will continue. Power is more important than collection of debts. This is the principle behind International Monetary Fund and World Bank loans to developing countries, to maintain them in a state of subservience and economic struggle so they can be ripe for exploitation by corporations from developed countries. Now, the masses of the USA population have been largely bankrupted, with no wage increases since the 1980s, two or more persons working to maintain one household, working more hours, less vacation time, etc. this is the desired outcome by the world power elite who want to control the world economy through financial subjugation, using military force (especially the US armed forces) only when needed. Financial subjugation is a viable means to subvert constitutions, governments and democracies, leaving them hollowed and powerless while appearing to offer some choice of handpicked politicians to the masses, an illusion.

The magnitude of the economic problems raises questions like what has been and continues to be the intent of the President and the congress? Did they not know that they should have assisted people with foreclosures and loss of jobs instead of helping the banks and "too big to fail" corporations with bailouts? These arguments were made by progressive politicians and economists but president Bush (Republican), with the recommendation of his advisors (including a former head of the investment firm Goldman Sacks (biggest contributors to the debacle), and Timothy Geithner (head of the New York Federal Reserve who did nothing to protest or stop the economic malfeasance that led to the debacle), chose to help the rich and president Obama (Democrat) chose to hire corporate democrat operatives from the Clinton administration (Larry Summers and Robert Rubin), and Timothy Geithner (head of the New York Federal Reserve) as his economic advisors, who actually pushed for laws that allowed the main debacle (bank malfeasance) to occur that led to the current disaster (compounding the already previously defunct USA economy). Those operatives had the same clients as those of the Bush administration, the rich and powerful corporations.

Even if we consider that their theory of helping banks and big businesses ("wealth effect") would trickle down to the masses was their intent, would not failure of 30 years of so called supply-side economics (Reaganomics, voodoo economics) have caused them to rethink their plans? As expected, the help to the rich, the banks and the too big to fail corporations did not do enough to help the masses and therefore the expected outcome of stagnation, high unemployment, etc. occurred and will continue to occur as long as that economic model continues to be employed. Up to now the "Tea Party" seems "hell bent" on stopping all spending by government, reducing government and dismantling governmental institutions like the education department and social security even though most Tea Party members receive social security assistance; ironic but also ignorant. If they wanted to have a profound effect on government they would work to ban all private contributions to congress members, a setup that constitutes legalized bribery. Then decisions and budgets would be more based on sound economics and ethics as opposed to corrupt politics. Otherwise, even if they were successful at reducing government, if the rules (Constitution) do not change, the same situation is bound to happen in future generations because the corrupt foundation of the government system (the Constitution) have not changed, only the cosmetics have changed; and that is no different from the politics of the past, therefore the "Tea Party" would be no different from the other parties but would merely be another smokescreen allowing the true rulers, the oligarchs to shield themselves from the public, another entity to blame for the miserable predicament of the society.

The Federal Reserve has attempted to control the economy via a theory called "Wealth Effect". The so called "wealth effect" is the idea that if they can cause bull markets (period of robust growth in stocks and commodities or other assets (for example: housing) the raised valuation of stocks and commodities will make people feel wealthy and thereby be willing to spend more money to sustain the economy (consumerism-buy things and sustain businesses that employ people) the "real economy" (economy of real people where exchange of goods takes place, unlike Wall Street). The "wealth effect" theory is nothing more than a variation of Reaganomics, "trickle down" economics, voodoo economics and has never worked in promoting real and sustainable benefits to the real economy of the middle and lower classes. The Federal Reserve tries to do this by controlling interest rates and printing money or contracting the money supply. By lowering interest rates the Federal Reserve is trying to cause people to invest in the stock market because the lower interest rates are providing almost no interest income, or negative income, if left in savings accounts. Quantitative Easing is simply the name given to the experiment of infusing massive quantities of money into the economy in order to prevent liquidity problems and bail out failing businesses (mainly big Wall Street banks). It has not worked, will not work and will hasten the devaluation of the US dollar and further weaken the economy and produce more bubbles (artificially inflated values due to too much liquidity that allows the rich to speculate and raise prices on stocks, commodities, houses, or anything else that might attract the interest of investors with more money to invest than they would normally have). During the creation of bubbles prices become overpriced, divorced from the true economic value, simply because investors are bidding up the prices. When the raised prices become unsustainable or there is no more liquidity to sustain the rising prices the bubble bursts and the value falls. The problem is not one of liquidity or interest rates but one of malfeasance, the corruption of the pseudo-capitalist economic model controlled by and for the benefit of corrupt banks and political system at the expense of the masses.

The actions of the Federal Reserve have and will weaken the US Dollar and may cause a currency war. If there is a currency war that may throw world economies into chaos and could lead to international conflicts. The Dollar bubble caused by Quantitative Easing by the Fed has caused a bubble in stocks and commodities (overpriced) and US Bonds (overpriced) which may burst at any time within the next 18 months. In the near term (1-4 years) we can expect more economic stagnation, high and or rising unemployment, social unrest (racial, gender, political and economic). If president Obama were to take the present defeat of the Democrats as a reason to fully go along with the main agendas of the Republicans, under the guise of "bipartisanship", this would enrage the Liberal/Progressive wing of the Democratic party which are already disheartened and angered by Obama's center-right politics that have caused many to regard him as a corporatist, a supporter of the corporate agenda over the well-being of the middle and lower classes (majority) due to policies (also advocated by right wing republican/conservative corporatists) such as continuation of wars, not fighting for single payer healthcare, not instituting real financial reform, authorizing political assassinations, not reinstating habeas corpus, bailouts, etc.). In the near and long term we can expect the housing market to stagnate and or fall further, unemployment rises and or stagnates and we can expect further increases in the value of gold as well as foreign currencies in relation to the US Dollar (especially those of countries that posses an abundance of natural resources) and more devaluation of the US Dollar leading to the cessation of its usage as the reserve currency of the world. If the current course remains we can also expect to see China and India take the place of the USA as the preeminent world economic powers. In the year 2008 China began to form an alternative world currency block, along with other Asian nations, to move away from the US Dollar and as that plan moves forward the US Dollar will lose its reserve status more and more and if the same malfeasance continues, the USA government's capacity to run huge deficits and sell treasury bonds to the world will go away, causing a full collapse of the economy; This all points to a stagnant USA economy for many years to come and the strong possibility of an economic downfall.

Finally, there is a very high probability that the economy of the USA will slip further into deep recession and depression especially since the government gridlock between Democrats and Republicans will prevent them from arriving at a proper solution (fiscal ethics, sound monetary policy, fair labor laws and trade policies) or even a temporary one, stimulus spending, leaving the Federal Reserve to print money that will inflate the dollar without providing any investment (infrastructure and or manufacturing base)- it has already and will be used by bankers to sure up their enterprises and bank accounts while investing in emerging markets. Thus, eventually they and other foreigners will follow the plan of buying assets on the cheap when the see that the economy has found a bottom (as occurred in March 2009) which will restart the next cycle of boom until the next bust... This period of downfall of assets will also temporarily affect all assets including gold and oil – commodities that are necessities. But it will present an investment/trading opportunity; when the immediate crisis passes there will be an opportunity to repurchase these again for wealth preservation purposes and for medium to long-term investment purposes.

NOTES

[i] http://en.wikipedia.org/wiki/White_paper

[ii] See the book *Introduction to Maat Philosophy* by Muata Ashby

[iii] http://www.youtube.com/watch?v=vVkFb26u9g8

[iv] http://www.usatoday.com/money/economy/2009-09-15-bernanke_N.htm

[v] http://www.youtube.com/watch?v=hq8XowRpQRI

[vi] "I don't think we're headed to a recession," President Bush said last Thursday (Feb. 28, 2007), echoing Fed Chief Bernanke's prediction to Congress that "the US economy will return to a strong growth path with price stability."

[vii] See the book *Dollar Crisis* for a more in depth look at the present crisis. See the book *THE COLLAPSE OF CIVILIZATION, The Roots of World Crises, The Death of American Empire* for a more in depth background of the Western economic system (crony Capitalism) and false democracy.

[viii] **The Coming Collapse of the Dollar and How to Profit From It** with James Turk, January 8, 2005 http://www.netcastdaily.com/broadcast/fsn2005-0108-2.asx

[ix] http://www.ccun.org/Opinion%20Editorials/2008/October/10%20o/Who%20Owns%20The%20Federal%20Reserve%20The%20Fed%20is%20privately%20owned.%20Its%20shareholders%20are%20private%20banks%20By%20Ellen%20Brown.htm

[x] (http://www.youtube.com/watch?v=KhEsqLcWHyA) (http://www.youtube.com/watch?v=koNXa2mXzGA&feature=quicklist) (http://www.calculatedriskblog.com/2009/05/new-mortgage-loan-reset-recast-chart.html)

[xi] (http://www.nytimes.com/1997/02/27/business/job-insecurity-of-workers-is-a-big-factor-in-fed-policy.html).

[xii] http://www.npr.org/templates/player/mediaPlayer.html?action=1&t=1&islist=false&id=99080028&m=99080011

[xiii] http://english.pravda.ru/world/americas/31-01-2006/75027-dollar-0

[xiv] http://www.dowjones.de/site/2009/09/world-bank-president-sees-other-reserve-currency-options-to-dollar.html

[xv] *The Creature from Jekyll Island: A Second Look at the Federal Reserve* by G. Edward Griffin

[xvi] *The Myth of Free Trade: The Pooring of America* by Ravi Batra

[xvii] **plu·toc·ra·cy** *n. pl.* **plu·toc·ra·cies** 1-Government by the wealthy. 2-A wealthy class that controls a government. 3-A government or state in which the wealthy rule.

[xviii] http://www.cbsnews.com/stories/2003/04/25/60minutes/main551091.shtml

---

[xix] **Homeowners frustrated by mortgage assistance program**

> http://www.cnn.com/2009/POLITICS/08/31/homeowners.mortgage/index.html?iref=newssearch

[xx] see the book: *THE COLLAPSE OF CIVILIZATION, The Roots of World Crises, The Death of American Empire*

[xxi]

> http://www.democracynow.org/2009/9/28/author_arundhati_roy_on_conflicts_and

[xxii] Discovered by Catherine Austin Fitts, Assistant Secretary of Housing
> http://www.financialsense.com/Experts/2004/AustinFitts.html

[xxiii] **Supercapitalism** was concept that developed in Italian Fascism.[1] In 1933, Benito Mussolini declared Italian Fascism's opposition to what he called "supercapitalism". Mussolini claimed that capitalism had degenerated. He also claimed that capitalism began with dynamic or heroic capitalism (1830-1870) followed by static capitalism (1870-1914) and then reaching its final form of decadent capitalism, known as supercapitalism, which began in 1914. (Falasca-Zamponi. Pp. 136.) Mussolini argued that Italian Fascism was in favour of dynamic and heroic capitalism for its contribution to industrialism and technical developments but claimed that it did not favour supercapitalism, which he claimed was incompatible with Italy's agricultural sector. (Falasca-Zamponi. 2000. Pp. 136.) Mussolini criticized this stage of supercapitalism, saying: "At this stage, supercapitalism finds its inspiration and its justification in a utopia: the utopia of unlimited consumption."

[xxiv] Mussolini criticized this stage of supercapitalism, saying: "Supercapitalism's ideal is the standardization of the human race from the cradle to the grave. Supercapitalism wants all babies to be born exactly the same length so that the cradles can be standardized and all children persuaded to like the same toys. It wants all men to don the very same uniform, to read the same book, to have the same tastes in films, and to desire the same so-called labor-saving devices. This is not the result of caprice. It inheres in the logic of events, for only thus can supercapitalism make its plans." Mussolini, Benito; Schnapp, Jeffery Thompson (ed.); Sears, Olivia E. (ed.); Stampino, Maria G. (ed.). "Address to the National Corporative Council (14 November 1933) and Senate Speech on the Bill Establishing the Corporations (abridged; 13 January 1934)". *A Primer of Italian Fascism.* University of Nebraska Press, 2000. Pp. 158.

[xxv] http://www.scribd.com/doc/6674234/Citigroup-Oct-16-2005-Plutonomy-Report-Part-1

[xxvi] ibid

[xxvii] ibid

[xxviii] Despite overwhelming public opposition, the Federal Communications Commission (FCC) has voted time after time in favor of relaxing media ownership limits. http://www.commoncause.org/site/pp.asp?c=dkLNK1MQIwG&b=4773655

[xxix] See the book *Collapse of Civilization and the Death of American Empire* by Muata Ashby

[xxx] http://www.scribd.com/doc/6674229/Citigroup-Mar-5-2006-Plutonomy-Report-Part-2?autodown=txt

[xxxi] Note by Ashby: (the crash of the economy in 2008 was an example of a policy error leading to asset deflation).

[xxxii]

http://www.telegraph.co.uk/finance/comment/ambroseevans_pritchard/3526645/Citigroup-says-gold-could-rise-above-2000-next-year-as-world-unravels.html

[xxxiii] *quantitative easing*- or *liquidity* is a theory and the application of it to counteract the economic downturn is an experiment.

[xxxiv] http://www.askbutwhy.com/2009/07/ravi-batra-on-thom-hartmann-show-07-24.html

[xxxv] http://www.investopedia.com/articles/economics/09/1970s-great-inflation.asp?partner=rss-recentarticles&viewed=1

[xxxvi] http://www.usdebtclock.org/

[xxxvii] Wall Street Words: An A to Z Guide to Investment Terms by David L. Scott. Copyright © 2003. Published by Houghton Mifflin.

[xxxviii] http://www.washingtonpost.com/wp-dyn/content/article/2009/03/13/AR2009031300703.html

[xxxix]

http://www.democracynow.org/blog/2008/9/19/current__reports_on_the_arrests_of_democracy_now_producers_at_the_republican_national_convention_in_st_paul

[xl] http://www.democracynow.org/2009/2/18/rnc_8

[xli] http://www.independent.co.uk/news/business/news/the-demise-of-the-dollar-1798175.html

[xlii] http://thegreatbustahead.com/

INDEX

RESORCES

The Sema Institute is not affiliated with the following firms. They are in business to legally assist those who would like to safeguard their assets and or acquire information and expertise to create sustainable lifestyles. This listing is not an endorsement by the Sema Institute. Before using any of the services below the reader is directed to investigate them and develop competent understanding of how their services work and how they can best make use of the services.

www.compactappliance.com

www.efoodsdirect.com

www.everbank.com/

www.goldmoney.com

www.internationalliving.com

www.jgam.com/

www.panamalaw.org/

www.parkseed.com/

www.prapanama.com/

www.sasa.ws/eng/contact.htm

www.seedsofchange.com/

www.solarcookers.org/basics/how.html

www.sovereignsociety.com

www.squarefootgardening.com/

www.sunoven.com/usa.asp

www.thalessecurities.com/

The Sema Institute

PO Box 570459

Miami, Fl. 33257

Other Books From C M Books

P.O.Box 570459
Miami, Florida, 33257
(305) 378-6253 Fax: (305) 378-6253

Prices subject to change.

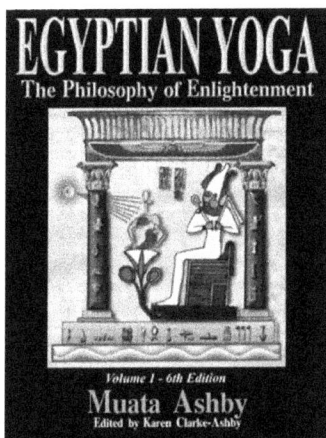

1. *EGYPTIAN YOGA: THE PHILOSOPHY OF ENLIGHTENMENT* An original, fully illustrated work, including hieroglyphs, detailing the meaning of the Egyptian mysteries, tantric yoga, psycho-spiritual and physical exercises. Egyptian Yoga is a guide to the practice of the highest spiritual philosophy which leads to absolute freedom from human misery and to immortality. It is well known by scholars that Egyptian philosophy is the basis of Western and Middle Eastern religious philosophies such as *Christianity, Islam, Judaism,* the *Kabala*, and Greek philosophy, but what about Indian philosophy, Yoga and Taoism? What were the original teachings? How can they be practiced today? What is the source of pain and suffering in the world and what is the solution? Discover the deepest mysteries of the mind and universe within and outside of yourself. 8.5" X 11" ISBN: 1-884564-01-1 Soft $19.95

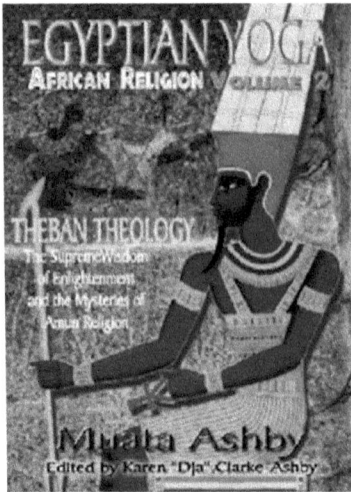

2.   *EGYPTIAN YOGA: African Religion Volume 2-* Theban
Theology U.S. In this long awaited sequel to *Egyptian Yoga:
The Philosophy of Enlightenment* you will take a fascinating
and enlightening journey back in time and discover the
teachings which constituted the epitome of Ancient Egyptian
spiritual wisdom. What are the disciplines which lead to the
fulfillment of all desires?   Delve into the three states of
consciousness (waking, dream and deep sleep) and the fourth
state which transcends them all, Neberdjer, "The Absolute."
These teachings of the city of Waset (Thebes) were the
crowning achievement of the Sages of Ancient Egypt. They
establish the standard mystical keys for understanding the
profound mystical symbolism of the Triad of human
consciousness. ISBN 1-884564-39-9 $23.95

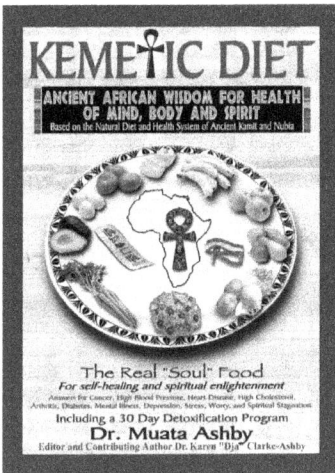

3.   *THE KEMETIC DIET: GUIDE TO HEALTH, DIET AND FASTING* Health issues have always been important to human beings since the beginning of time. The earliest records of history show that the art of healing was held in high esteem since the time of Ancient Egypt. In the early 20th century, medical doctors had almost attained the status of sainthood by the promotion of the idea that they alone were "scientists" while other healing modalities and traditional healers who did not follow the "scientific method' were nothing but superstitious, ignorant charlatans who at best would take the money of their clients and at worst kill them with the unscientific "snake oils" and "irrational theories". In the late 20th century, the failure of the modern medical establishment's ability to lead the general public to good health, promoted the move by many in society towards "alternative medicine". Alternative medicine disciplines are those healing modalities which do not adhere to the philosophy of allopathic medicine. Allopathic medicine is what medical doctors practice by an large. It is the theory that disease is caused by agencies outside the body such as bacteria, viruses or physical means which affect the body. These can therefore be treated by medicines and therapies   The natural healing method began in the absence of extensive technologies with the idea that all the answers for health may be found in nature or rather, the deviation from nature. Therefore, the health of the body can be restored by correcting the aberration and thereby restoring balance. This is the area that will be covered in this volume. Allopathic techniques have their place in the art of healing.

However, we should not forget that the body is a grand achievement of the spirit and built into it is the capacity to maintain itself and heal itself. Ashby, Muata ISBN: 1-884564-49-6 $28.95

4.   INITIATION INTO EGYPTIAN YOGA Shedy: Spiritual discipline or program, to go deeply into the mysteries, to study the mystery teachings and literature profoundly, to penetrate the mysteries. You will learn about the mysteries of initiation into the teachings and practice of Yoga and how to become an Initiate of the mystical sciences. This insightful manual is the first in a series which introduces you to the goals of daily spiritual and yoga practices: Meditation, Diet, Words of Power and the ancient wisdom teachings.   8.5" X 11" ISBN 1-884564-02-X   Soft Cover $24.95 U.S.

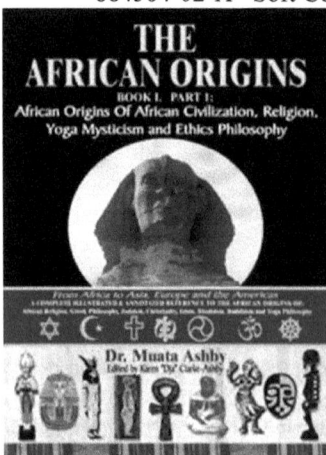

5.   *THE AFRICAN ORIGINS OF CIVILIZATION, RELIGION
AND YOGA SPIRITUALITY AND ETHICS PHILOSOPHY*
HARD COVER EDITION Part 1, Part 2, Part 3 in one volume
683 Pages Hard Cover First Edition Three volumes in one.
Over the past several years I have been asked to put together
in one volume the most important evidences showing the
correlations and common teachings between Kamitan
(Ancient Egyptian) culture and religion and that of India. The
questions of the history of Ancient Egypt, and the latest
archeological evidences showing civilization and culture in
Ancient Egypt and its spread to other countries, has intrigued
many scholars as well as mystics over the years. Also, the
possibility that Ancient Egyptian Priests and Priestesses
migrated to Greece, India and other countries to carry on the
traditions of the Ancient Egyptian Mysteries, has been
speculated over the years as well. In chapter 1 of the book
Egyptian Yoga The Philosophy of Enlightenment, 1995, I first
introduced the deepest comparison between Ancient Egypt
and India that had been brought forth up to that time. Now, in
the year 2001 this new book, *THE AFRICAN ORIGINS OF
CIVILIZATION, MYSTICAL RELIGION AND YOGA
PHILOSOPHY,* more fully explores the motifs, symbols and
philosophical correlations between Ancient Egyptian and
Indian mysticism and clearly shows not only that Ancient
Egypt and India were connected culturally but also spiritually.
How does this knowledge help the spiritual aspirant? This
discovery has great importance for the Yogis and mystics who
follow the philosophy of Ancient Egypt and the mysticism of
India. It means that India has a longer history and heritage
than was previously understood. It shows that the mysteries of
Ancient Egypt were essentially a yoga tradition which did not
die but rather developed into the modern day systems of Yoga
technology of India. It further shows that African culture
developed Yoga Mysticism earlier than any other civilization
in history. All of this expands our understanding of the unity
of culture and the deep legacy of Yoga, which stretches into
the distant past, beyond the Indus Valley civilization, the
earliest known high culture in India as well as the Vedic
tradition of Aryan culture. Therefore, Yoga culture and
mysticism is the oldest known tradition of spiritual
development and Indian mysticism is an extension of the
Ancient Egyptian mysticism. By understanding the legacy
which Ancient Egypt gave to India the mysticism of India is

better understood and by comprehending the heritage of Indian Yoga, which is rooted in Ancient Egypt the Mysticism of Ancient Egypt is also better understood. This expanded understanding allows us to prove the underlying kinship of humanity, through the common symbols, motifs and philosophies which are not disparate and confusing teachings but in reality expressions of the same study of truth through metaphysics and mystical realization of Self. (HARD COVER) ISBN: 1-884564-50-X $45.00 U.S.   81/2" X 11"

6. *AFRICAN ORIGINS BOOK 1 PART 1* African Origins of African Civilization, Religion, Yoga Mysticism and Ethics Philosophy-Soft Cover $24.95 ISBN: 1-884564-55-0

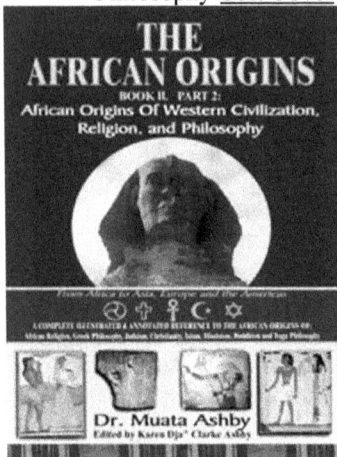

7. *AFRICAN ORIGINS BOOK 2 PART 2* African Origins of Western Civilization, Religion and Philosophy (Soft) -Soft Cover $24.95 ISBN: 1-884564-56-9

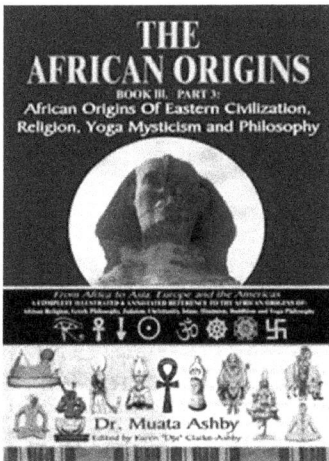

8.   *EGYPT AND INDIA* AFRICAN ORIGINS OF *Eastern Civilization, Religion, Yoga Mysticism and Philosophy-*Soft Cover $29.95 (Soft) ISBN: 1-884564-57-7

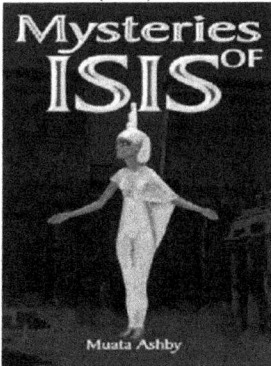

9.   *THE MYSTERIES OF ISIS:* **The Ancient Egyptian Philosophy of Self-Realization** - There are several paths to discover the Divine and the mysteries of the higher Self. This volume details the mystery teachings of the goddess Aset (Isis) from Ancient Egypt- the path of wisdom. It includes the teachings of her temple and the disciplines that are enjoined for the initiates of the temple of Aset as they were given in ancient times. Also, this book includes the teachings of the main myths of Aset that lead a human being to spiritual enlightenment and immortality. Through the study of ancient myth and the illumination of initiatic understanding the idea of God is expanded from the mythological comprehension to the metaphysical. Then this metaphysical understanding is related

to you, the student, so as to begin understanding your true divine nature. ISBN 1-884564-24-0 $22.99

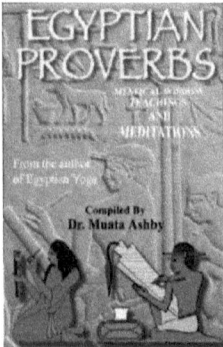

10.   *EGYPTIAN PROVERBS:* collection of —Ancient Egyptian Proverbs and Wisdom Teachings -How to live according to MAAT Philosophy. Beginning Meditation. All proverbs are indexed for easy searches. For the first time in one volume, — —Ancient Egyptian Proverbs, wisdom teachings and meditations, fully illustrated with hieroglyphic text and symbols. EGYPTIAN PROVERBS is a unique collection of knowledge and wisdom which you can put into practice today and transform your life. $14.95 U.S   ISBN: 1-884564-00-3

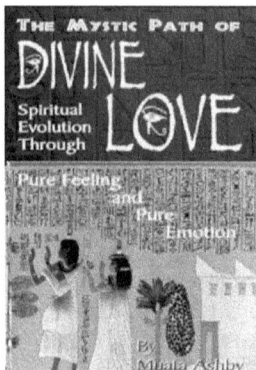

11.   *GOD OF LOVE: THE PATH OF DIVINE LOVE The Process of Mystical Transformation and The Path of Divine Love* This Volume focuses on the ancient wisdom teachings of "Neter Merri" –the Ancient Egyptian philosophy of Divine Love and how to use them in a scientific process for self-transformation. Love is one of the most powerful human

emotions. It is also the source of Divine feeling that unifies God and the individual human being. When love is fragmented and diminished by egoism the Divine connection is lost. The Ancient tradition of Neter Merri leads human beings back to their Divine connection, allowing them to discover their innate glorious self that is actually Divine and immortal. This volume will detail the process of transformation from ordinary consciousness to cosmic consciousness through the integrated practice of the teachings and the path of Devotional Love toward the Divine. 5.5"x 8.5" ISBN 1-884564-11-9 $22.95

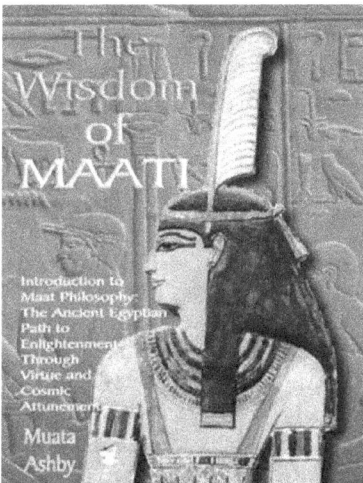

12.   INTRODUCTION TO MAAT PHILOSOPHY: *Spiritual Enlightenment Through the Path of Virtue*   Known commonly as Karma in India, the teachings of MAAT contain an extensive philosophy based on ariu (deeds) and their fructification in the form of shai and renenet (fortune and destiny, leading to Meskhenet (fate in a future birth) for living virtuously and with orderly wisdom are explained and the student is to begin practicing the precepts of Maat in daily life so as to promote the process of purification of the heart in preparation for the judgment of the soul. This judgment will be understood not as an event that will occur at the time of death but as an event that occurs continuously, at every moment in the life of the individual. The student will learn how to become allied with the forces of the Higher Self and to thereby begin cleansing the mind (heart) of impurities so as to attain a higher vision of reality. ISBN 1-884564-20-8 $22.99

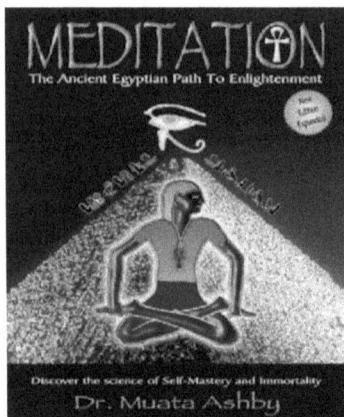

13.   *MEDITATION The Ancient Egyptian Path to Enlightenment*
Many people do not know about the rich history of meditation
practice in Ancient Egypt. This volume outlines the theory of
meditation and presents the Ancient Egyptian Hieroglyphic
text which give instruction as to the nature of the mind and its
three modes of expression. It also presents the texts which
give instruction on the practice of meditation for spiritual
Enlightenment and unity with the Divine. This volume allows
the reader to begin practicing meditation by explaining, in
easy to understand terms, the simplest form of meditation and
working up to the most advanced form which was practiced in
ancient times and which is still practiced by yogis around the
world in modern times. ISBN 1-884564-27-7 $22.99

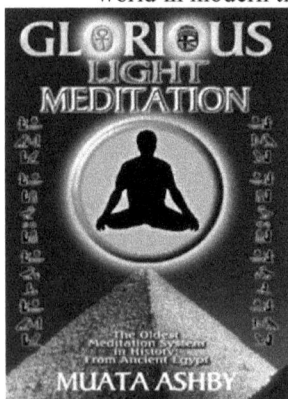

14.   *THE GLORIOUS LIGHT MEDITATION* TECHNIQUE OF
ANCIENT EGYPT New for the year 2000. This volume is based
on the earliest known instruction in history given for the

practice of formal meditation. Discovered by Dr. Muata Ashby, it is inscribed on the walls of the Tomb of Seti I in Thebes Egypt. This volume details the philosophy and practice of this unique system of meditation originated in Ancient Egypt and the earliest practice of meditation known in the world which occurred in the most advanced African Culture. ISBN: 1-884564-15-1 $16.95 (PB)

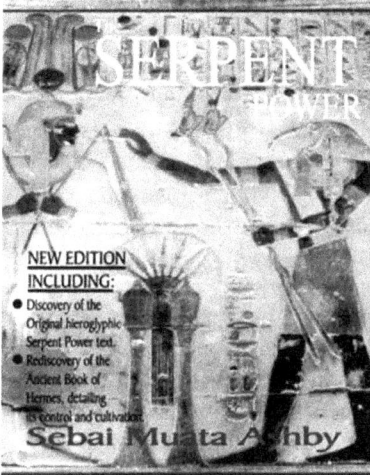

NEW EDITION INCLUDING:
• Discovery of the Original hieroglyphic Serpent Power text.
• Rediscovery of the Ancient Book of Hermes, detailing its control and cultivation

Sebai Muata Ashby

15.   *THE SERPENT POWER: The Ancient Egyptian Mystical Wisdom of the Inner Life Force.*   This Volume specifically deals with the latent life Force energy of the universe and in the human body, its control and sublimation. How to develop the Life Force energy of the subtle body. This Volume will introduce the esoteric wisdom of the science of how virtuous living acts in a subtle and mysterious way to cleanse the latent psychic energy conduits and vortices of the spiritual body. ISBN 1-884564-19-4 $22.95

16. *EGYPTIAN YOGA The Postures of The Gods and Goddesses*
Discover the physical postures and exercises practiced thousands of years ago in Ancient Egypt which are today known as Yoga exercises. Discover the history of the postures and how they were transferred from Ancient Egypt in Africa to India through Buddhist Tantrism. Then practice the postures as you discover the mythic teaching that originally gave birth to the postures and was practiced by the Ancient Egyptian priests and priestesses. This work is based on the pictures and teachings from the Creation story of Ra, The Asarian Resurrection Myth and the carvings and reliefs from various Temples in Ancient Egypt 8.5" X 11" ISBN 1-884564-10-0 Soft Cover $21.95   Exercise video $20

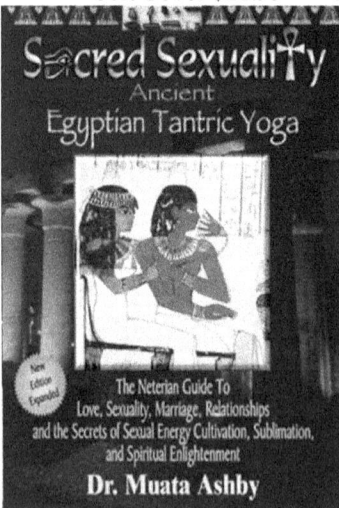

17.   *SACRED SEXUALITY: ANCIENT EGYPTIAN TANTRA YOGA: The Art of Sex* Sublimation and Universal Consciousness This Volume will expand on the male and female principles within the human body and in the universe and further detail the sublimation of sexual energy into spiritual energy. The student will study the deities Min and Hathor, Asar and Aset, Geb and Nut and discover the mystical implications for a practical spiritual discipline. This Volume will also focus on the Tantric aspects of Ancient Egyptian and Indian mysticism, the purpose of sex and the mystical teachings of sexual sublimation which lead to self-knowledge and Enlightenment. ISBN 1-884564-03-8 $24.95

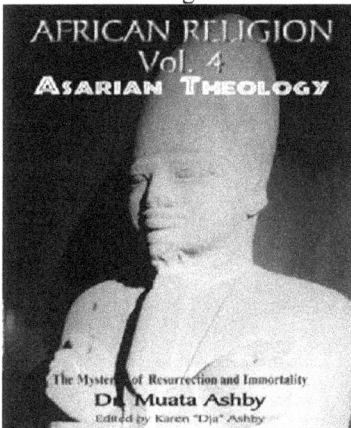

AFRICAN RELIGION Vol. 4
ASARIAN THEOLOGY
The Mystery of Resurrection and Immortality
Dr. Muata Ashby
Edited by Karen "Dja" Ashby

18.   *AFRICAN RELIGION Volume 4: ASARIAN THEOLOGY: RESURRECTING OSIRIS* The path of Mystical Awakening and the Keys to Immortality NEW REVISED AND EXPANDED EDITION! The Ancient Sages created stories based on human and superhuman beings whose struggles, aspirations, needs and desires ultimately lead them to discover their true Self. The myth of Aset, Asar and Heru is no exception in this area. While there is no one source where the entire story may be found, pieces of it are inscribed in various ancient Temples walls, tombs, steles and papyri. For the first time available, the complete myth of Asar, Aset and Heru has been compiled from original Ancient Egyptian, Greek and Coptic Texts. This epic myth has been richly illustrated with reliefs from the Temple of Heru at Edfu, the Temple of Aset at Philae, the Temple of Asar at Abydos, the Temple of Hathor at Denderah and various papyri, inscriptions and reliefs. Discover the myth which inspired the teachings of the *Shetaut*

Neter (Egyptian Mystery System - Egyptian Yoga) and the Egyptian Book of Coming Forth By Day. Also, discover the three levels of Ancient Egyptian Religion, how to understand the mysteries of the Duat or Astral World and how to discover the abode of the Supreme in the Amenta, *The Other World* The ancient religion of Asar, Aset and Heru, if properly understood, contains all of the elements necessary to lead the sincere aspirant to attain immortality through inner self-discovery. This volume presents the entire myth and explores the main mystical themes and rituals associated with the myth for understating human existence, creation and the way to achieve spiritual emancipation - *Resurrection.* The Asarian myth is so powerful that it influenced and is still having an effect on the major world religions. Discover the origins and mystical meaning of the Christian Trinity, the Eucharist ritual and the ancient origin of the birthday of Jesus Christ. Soft Cover ISBN: 1-884564-27-5 $24.95

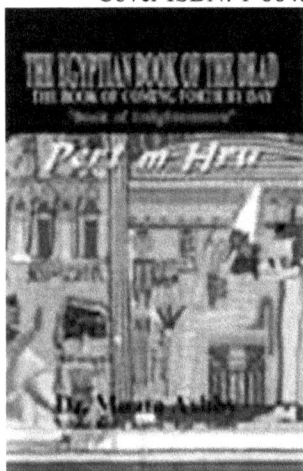

19.   *THE EGYPTIAN BOOK OF THE DEAD MYSTICISM OF THE PERT EM HERU* " I Know myself, I know myself, I am One With God!–From the Pert Em Heru "The Ru Pert em Heru" or "Ancient Egyptian Book of The Dead," or "Book of Coming Forth By Day" as it is more popularly known, has fascinated the world since the successful translation of Ancient Egyptian hieroglyphic scripture over 150 years ago. The astonishing writings in it reveal that the Ancient Egyptians believed in life after death and in an ultimate destiny to discover the Divine. The elegance and aesthetic beauty of the hieroglyphic text itself has inspired many see it

as an art form in and of itself. But is there more to it than that? Did the Ancient Egyptian wisdom contain more than just aphorisms and hopes of eternal life beyond death? In this volume Dr. Muata Ashby, the author of over 25 books on Ancient Egyptian Yoga Philosophy has produced a new translation of the original texts which uncovers a mystical teaching underlying the sayings and rituals instituted by the Ancient Egyptian Sages and Saints. "Once the philosophy of Ancient Egypt is understood as a mystical tradition instead of as a religion or primitive mythology, it reveals its secrets which if practiced today will lead anyone to discover the glory of spiritual self-discovery. The Pert em Heru is in every way comparable to the Indian Upanishads or the Tibetan Book of the Dead." $28.95   ISBN# 1-884564-28-3 Size: 8½" X 11

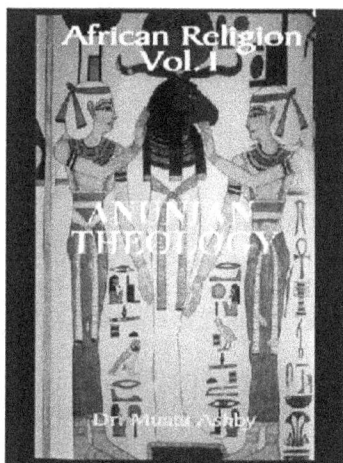

20.   *African Religion VOL. 1- ANUNIAN THEOLOGY THE MYSTERIES OF RA* The Philosophy of Anu and The Mystical Teachings of The Ancient Egyptian Creation Myth Discover the mystical teachings contained in the Creation Myth and the gods and goddesses who brought creation and human beings into existence. The Creation myth of Anu is the source of Anunian Theology but also of the other main theological systems of Ancient Egypt that also influenced other world religions including Christianity, Hinduism and Buddhism. The Creation Myth holds the key to understanding the universe and for attaining spiritual Enlightenment. ISBN: 1-884564-38-0 $19.95

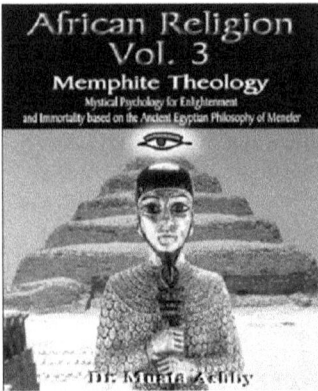

21.   *African Religion VOL 3: Memphite Theology: MYSTERIES OF MIND* Mystical Psychology & Mental Health for Enlightenment and Immortality based on the Ancient Egyptian Philosophy of Menefer -Mysticism of Ptah, Egyptian Physics and Yoga Metaphysics and the Hidden properties of Matter. This volume uncovers the mystical psychology of the Ancient Egyptian wisdom teachings centering on the philosophy of the Ancient Egyptian city of Menefer (Memphite Theology). How to understand the mind and how to control the senses and lead the mind to health, clarity and mystical self-discovery. This Volume will also go deeper into the philosophy of God as creation and will explore the concepts of modern science and how they correlate with ancient teachings. This Volume will lay the ground work for the understanding of the philosophy of universal consciousness and the initiatic/yogic insight into who or what is God? ISBN 1-884564-07-0 $22.95

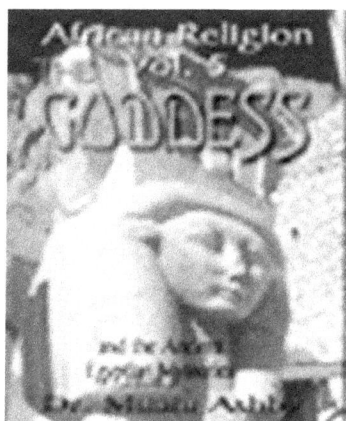

22.   *AFRICAN RELIGION VOLUME 5: THE GODDESS AND THE EGYPTIAN MYSTERIESTHE PATH OF THE GODDESS THE GODDESS PATH* The Secret Forms of the Goddess and the Rituals of Resurrection The Supreme Being may be worshipped as father or as mother. *Ushet Rekhat* or *Mother Worship*, is the spiritual process of worshipping the Divine in the form of the Divine Goddess. It celebrates the most important forms of the Goddess including *Nathor, Maat, Aset, Arat, Amentet and Hathor* and explores their mystical meaning as well as the rising of *Sirius,* the star of Aset (Aset) and the new birth of Hor (Heru). The end of the year is a time of reckoning, reflection and engendering a new or renewed positive movement toward attaining spiritual Enlightenment. The Mother Worship devotional meditation ritual, performed on five days during the month of December and on New Year's Eve, is based on the Ushet Rekhit. During the ceremony, the cosmic forces, symbolized by Sirius - and the constellation of Orion ---, are harnessed through the understanding and devotional attitude of the participant. This propitiation draws the light of wisdom and health to all those who share in the ritual, leading to prosperity and wisdom. $14.95 ISBN 1-884564-18-6

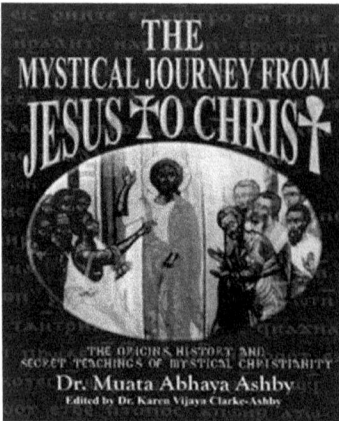

23.   *THE MYSTICAL JOURNEY FROM JESUS TO CHRIST*
Discover the ancient Egyptian origins of Christianity before
the Catholic Church and learn the mystical teachings given by
Jesus to assist all humanity in becoming Christlike. Discover
the secret meaning of the Gospels that were discovered in
Egypt. Also discover how and why so many Christian
churches came into being. Discover that the Bible still holds
the keys to mystical realization even though its original
writings were changed by the church. Discover how to
practice the original teachings of Christianity which leads to
the Kingdom of Heaven. $24.95   ISBN# 1-884564-05-4
size: 8½" X 11"

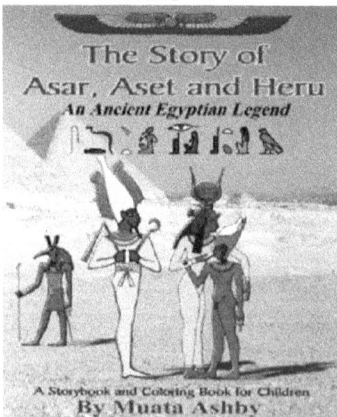

24.   *THE STORY OF ASAR, ASET AND HERU:* An Ancient
Egyptian Legend (For Children)   Now for the first time, the
most ancient myth of Ancient Egypt comes alive for children.
Inspired by the books *The Asarian Resurrection: The Ancient*

Egyptian Bible and *The Mystical Teachings of The Asarian Resurrection, The Story of Asar, Aset and Heru* is an easy to understand and thrilling tale which inspired the children of Ancient Egypt to aspire to greatness and righteousness. If you and your child have enjoyed stories like *The Lion King* and *Star Wars you will love The Story of Asar, Aset and Heru.* Also, if you know the story of Jesus and Krishna you will discover than Ancient Egypt had a similar myth and that this myth carries important spiritual teachings for living a fruitful and fulfilling life. This book may be used along with *The Parents Guide To The Asarian Resurrection Myth: How to Teach Yourself and Your Child the Principles of Universal Mystical Religion.* The guide provides some background to the Asarian Resurrection myth and it also gives insight into the mystical teachings contained in it which you may introduce to your child. It is designed for parents who wish to grow spiritually with their children and it serves as an introduction for those who would like to study the Asarian Resurrection Myth in depth and to practice its teachings. 8.5" X 11" ISBN: 1-884564-31-3 $12.95

25.   *THE PARENTS GUIDE TO THE AUSARIAN RESURRECTION MYTH:* How to Teach Yourself and Your Child the Principles of Universal Mystical Religion. This insightful manual brings for the timeless wisdom of the ancient through the Ancient Egyptian myth of Asar, Aset and Heru and the mystical teachings contained in it for parents who want to guide their children to understand and practice the teachings of mystical spirituality. This manual may be used with the children's storybook *The Story of Asar, Aset and*

Heru by Dr. Muata Abhaya Ashby.   ISBN: 1-884564-30-5
$16.95

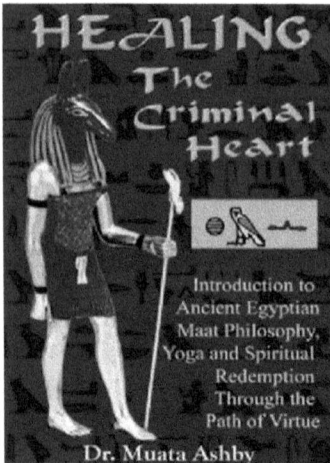

26.   *HEALING THE CRIMINAL HEART.* Introduction to Maat Philosophy, Yoga and Spiritual Redemption Through the Path of Virtue   Who is a criminal? Is there such a thing as a criminal heart? What is the source of evil and sinfulness and is there any way to rise above it? Is there redemption for those who have committed sins, even the worst crimes?   Ancient Egyptian mystical psychology holds important answers to these questions. Over ten thousand years ago mystical psychologists, the Sages of Ancient Egypt, studied and charted the human mind and spirit and laid out a path which will lead to spiritual redemption, prosperity and Enlightenment.   This introductory volume brings forth the teachings of the Asarian Resurrection, the most important myth of Ancient Egypt, with relation to the faults of human existence: anger, hatred, greed, lust, animosity, discontent, ignorance, egoism jealousy, bitterness, and a myriad of psycho-spiritual ailments which keep a human being in a state of negativity and adversity ISBN: 1-884564-17-8 $15.95

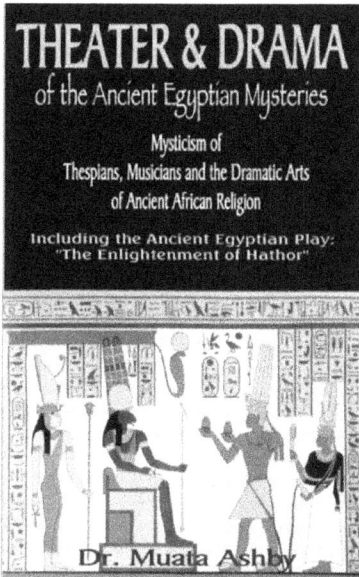

THEATER & DRAMA
of the Ancient Egyptian Mysteries

Mysticism of
Thespians, Musicians and the Dramatic Arts
of Ancient African Religion

Including the Ancient Egyptian Play:
"The Enlightenment of Hathor"

Dr. Muata Ashby

27.   *TEMPLE RITUAL OF THE ANCIENT EGYPTIAN MYSTERIES--THEATER & DRAMA OF THE ANCIENT EGYPTIAN MYSTERIES*: Details the practice of the mysteries and ritual program of the temple and the philosophy an practice of the ritual of the mysteries, its purpose and execution. Featuring the Ancient Egyptian stage play-"The Enlightenment of Hathor' Based on an Ancient Egyptian Drama, The original Theater -Mysticism of the Temple of Hetheru 1-884564-14-3 $19.95 By Dr. Muata Ashby

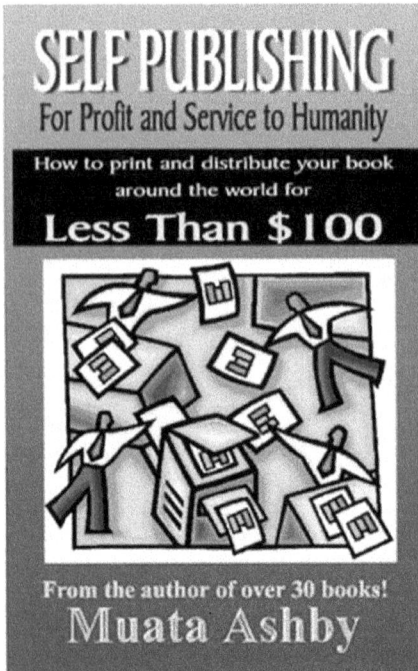

SELF PUBLISHING
For Profit and Service to Humanity
How to print and distribute your book
around the world for
Less Than $100

From the author of over 30 books!
Muata Ashby

28.   *GUIDE TO PRINT ON DEMAND: SELF-PUBLISH FOR PROFIT,*
SPIRITUAL FULFILLMENT AND SERVICE TO HUMANITY
Everyone asks us how we produced so many books in such a
short time. Here are the secrets to writing and producing books
that uplift humanity and how to get them printed for a fraction
of the regular cost. Anyone can become an author even if they
have limited funds. All that is necessary is the willingness to
learn how the printing and book business work and the desire
to follow the special instructions given here for preparing your
manuscript format. Then you take your work directly to the
non-traditional companies who can produce your books for
less than the traditional book printer can. ISBN: 1-884564-40-
2      $16.95 U. S.

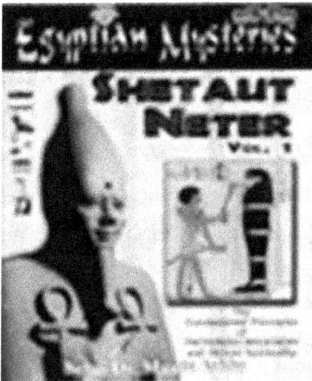

29.   *Egyptian Mysteries: Vol. 1,* Shetaut Neter What are the Mysteries? For thousands of years the spiritual tradition of Ancient Egypt, S*hetaut Neter,* "The Egyptian Mysteries," "The Secret Teachings," have fascinated, tantalized and amazed the world. At one time exalted and recognized as the highest culture of the world, by Africans, Europeans, Asiatics, Hindus, Buddhists and other cultures of the ancient world, in time it was shunned by the emerging orthodox world religions. Its temples desecrated, its philosophy maligned, its tradition spurned, its philosophy dormant in the mystical *Medu Neter,* the mysterious hieroglyphic texts which hold the secret symbolic meaning that has scarcely been discerned up to now. What are the secrets of *Nehast* {spiritual awakening and emancipation, resurrection}. More than just a literal translation, this volume is for awakening to the secret code *Shetitu* of the teaching which was not deciphered by Egyptologists, nor could be understood by ordinary spiritualists. This book is a reinstatement of the original science made available for our times, to the reincarnated followers of Ancient Egyptian culture and the prospect of spiritual freedom to break the bonds of *Khemn,* "ignorance," and slavery to evil forces: *Såaa* . ISBN: 1-884564-41-0 $19.99

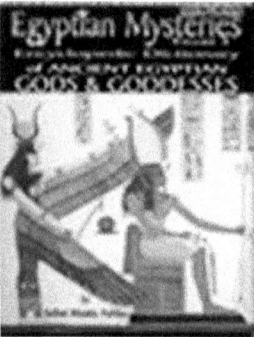

30.   *EGYPTIAN MYSTERIES VOL 2:* Dictionary of Gods and Goddesses This book is about the mystery of neteru, the gods and goddesses of Ancient Egypt (Kamit, Kemet). Neteru means "Gods and Goddesses." But the Neterian teaching of Neteru represents more than the usual limited modern day concept of "divinities" or "spirits." The Neteru of Kamit are also metaphors, cosmic principles and vehicles for the enlightening teachings of Shetaut Neter (Ancient Egyptian-African Religion). Actually they are the elements for one of the most advanced systems of spirituality ever conceived in human history. Understanding the concept of neteru provides a firm basis for spiritual evolution and the pathway for viable culture, peace on earth and a healthy human society.   Why is it important to have gods and goddesses in our lives? In order for spiritual evolution to be possible, once a human being has accepted that there is existence after death and there is a transcendental being who exists beyond time and space knowledge, human beings need a connection to that which transcends the ordinary experience of human life in time and space and a means to understand the transcendental reality beyond the mundane reality. ISBN: 1-884564-23-2 $21.95

31.   *EGYPTIAN MYSTERIES VOL. 3* The Priests and Priestesses of Ancient Egypt This volume details the path of Neterian priesthood, the joys, challenges and rewards of advanced Neterian life, the teachings that allowed the priests and priestesses to manage the most long lived civilization in human history and how that path can be adopted today; for those who want to tread the path of the Clergy of Shetaut Neter. ISBN: 1-884564-53-4 $24.95

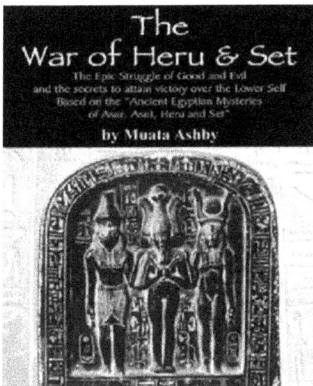

32.   *The War of Heru and Set:* The Struggle of Good and Evil for Control of the World and The Human Soul This volume contains a novelized version of the Asarian Resurrection myth that is based on the actual scriptures presented in the Book Asarian Religion (old name –Resurrecting Osiris). This volume is prepared in the form of a screenplay and can be easily adapted to be used as a stage play. Spiritual seeking is a mythic journey that has many emotional highs and lows, ecstasies and depressions, victories and frustrations. This is the War of Life that is played out in the myth as the struggle of Heru and Set and those are mythic characters that represent the human Higher and Lower self. How to understand the war and emerge victorious in the journey o life? The ultimate victory and fulfillment can be experienced, which is not changeable or lost in time. The purpose of myth is to convey the wisdom of life through the story of divinities who show the way to overcome the challenges and foibles of life. In this volume the feelings and emotions of the characters of the myth have been highlighted to show the deeply rich texture of the Ancient Egyptian myth. This myth contains deep spiritual teachings and insights into the nature of self, of God and the mysteries of life and the means to discover the true meaning of

life and thereby achieve the true purpose of life. To become victorious in the battle of life means to become the King (or Queen) of Egypt.Have you seen movies like The Lion King, Hamlet, The Odyssey, or The Little Buddha? These have been some of the most popular movies in modern times. The Sema Institute of Yoga is dedicated to researching and presenting the wisdom and culture of ancient Africa. The Script is designed to be produced as a motion picture but may be addapted for the theater as well. $21.95   copyright 1998 By Dr. Muata Ashby ISBN 1-8840564-44-5

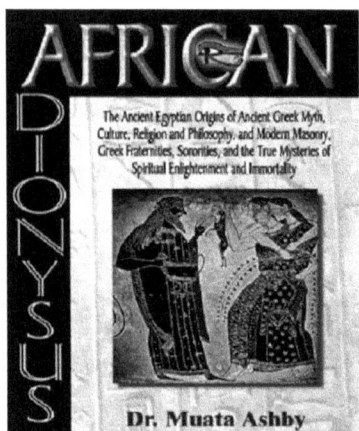

33.   *AFRICAN DIONYSUS: FROM EGYPT TO GREECE:* The Kamitan Origins of Greek Culture and Religion ISBN: 1-884564-47-X   FROM EGYPT TO GREECE   This insightful manual is a reference to Ancient Egyptian mythology and philosophy and its correlation to what later became known as Greek and Rome mythology and philosophy. It outlines the basic tenets of the mythologies and shoes the ancient origins of Greek culture in Ancient Egypt. This volume also documents the origins of the Greek alphabet in Egypt as well as Greek religion, myth and philosophy of the gods and goddesses from Egypt from the myth of Atlantis and archaic period with the Minoans to the Classical period. This volume also acts as a resource for Colleges students who would like to set up fraternities and sororities based on the original Ancient Egyptian principles of Sheti and Maat philosophy. ISBN: 1-884564-47-X $22.95 U.S.

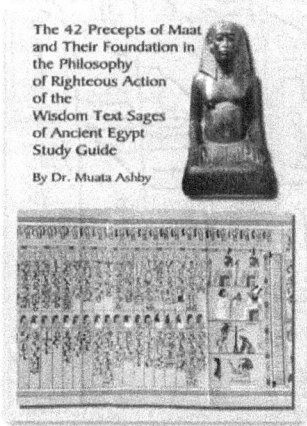

34. *THE FORTY TWO PRECEPTS OF MAAT, THE PHILOSOPHY OF RIGHTEOUS ACTION AND THE ANCIENT EGYPTIAN WISDOM TEXTS* <u>ADVANCED STUDIES</u> This manual is designed for use with the 1998 Maat Philosophy Class conducted by Dr. Muata Ashby. This is a detailed study of Maat Philosophy. It contains a compilation of the 42 laws or precepts of Maat and the corresponding principles which they represent along with the teachings of the ancient Egyptian Sages relating to each. Maat philosophy was the basis of Ancient Egyptian society and government as well as the heart of Ancient Egyptian myth and spirituality. Maat is at once a goddess, a cosmic force and a living social doctrine, which promotes social harmony and thereby paves the way for spiritual evolution in all levels of society. ISBN: 1-884564-48-8 $16.95 U.S.

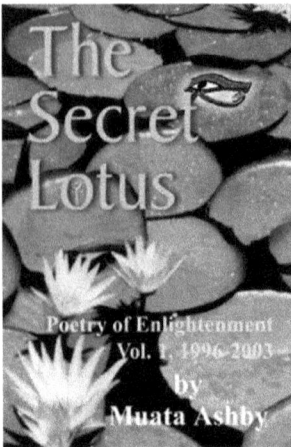

35.   THE SECRET LOTUS: Poetry of Enlightenment
Discover the mystical sentiment of the Kemetic teaching as expressed through the poetry of Sebai Muata Ashby. The teaching of spiritual awakening is uniquely experienced when the poetic sensibility is present. This first volume contains the poems written between 1996 and 2003. **1-884564--16 -X $16.99**

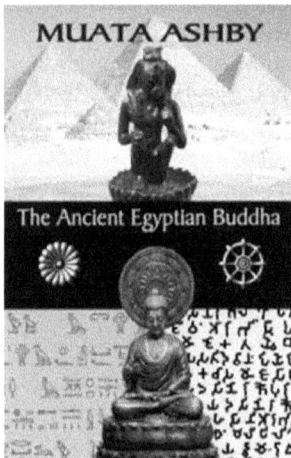

36. The Ancient Egyptian Buddha: The Ancient Egyptian Origins of Buddhism
This book is a compilation of several sections of a larger work, a book by the name of African Origins of Civilization, Religion, Yoga Mysticism and Ethics Philosophy. It also contains some additional evidences not contained in the larger work that demonstrate the correlation between Ancient Egyptian Religion and Buddhism. This

book is one of several compiled short volumes that has been compiled so as to facilitate access to specific subjects contained in the larger work which is over 680 pages long. These short and small volumes have been specifically designed to cover one subject in a brief and low cost format. This present volume, The Ancient Egyptian Buddha: The Ancient Egyptian Origins of Buddhism, formed one subject in the larger work; actually it was one chapter of the larger work. However, this volume has some new additional evidences and comparisons of Buddhist and Neterian (Ancient Egyptian) philosophies not previously discussed. It was felt that this subject needed to be discussed because even in the early 21st century, the idea persists that Buddhism originated only in India independently. Yet there is ample evidence from ancient writings and perhaps more importantly, iconographical evidences from the Ancient Egyptians and early Buddhists themselves that prove otherwise. This handy volume has been designed to be accessible to young adults and all others who would like to have an easy reference with documentation on this important subject. This is an important subject because the frame of reference with which we look at a culture depends strongly on our conceptions about its origins. in this case, if we look at the Buddhism as an Asiatic religion we would treat it and it's culture in one way. If we id as African [Ancient Egyptian] we not only would see it in a different light but we also must ascribe Africa with a glorious legacy that matches any other culture in human history and gave rise to one of the present day most important religious philosophies. We would also look at the culture and philosophies of the Ancient Egyptians as having African insights that offer us greater depth into the Buddhist philosophies. Those insights inform our knowledge about other African traditions and we can also begin to understand in a deeper way the effect of Ancient Egyptian culture on African culture and also on the Asiatic as well. We would also be able to discover the glorious and wondrous teaching of mystical philosophy that Ancient Egyptian Shetaut Neter religion offers, that is as powerful as any other mystic system of spiritual philosophy in the world today. ISBN: 1-884564-61-5 $28 95

Reginald Muata Ashby

37. The Death of American Empire: Neo-conservatism, Theocracy, Economic Imperialism, Environmental Disaster and the Collapse of Civilization

This work is a collection of essays relating to social and economic, leadership, and ethics, ecological and religious issues that are facing the world today in order to understand the course of history that has led humanity to its present condition and then arrive at positive solutions that will lead to better outcomes for all humanity. It surveys the development and decline of major empires throughout history and focuses on the creation of American Empire along with the social, political and economic policies that led to the prominence of the United States of America as a Superpower including the rise of the political control of the neo-con political philosophy including militarism and the military industrial complex in American politics and the rise of the religious right into and American Theocracy movement. This volume details, through historical and current events, the psychology behind the dominance of western culture in world politics through the "Superpower Syndrome Mandatory Conflict Complex" that drives the Superpower culture to establish itself above all others and then act hubristically to dominate world culture through legitimate influences as well as coercion, media censorship and misinformation leading to international hegemony and world conflict. This volume also details the financial policies that gave rise to American prominence in the global economy, especially after World War II, and promoted American preeminence over the world economy through Globalization as well as the environmental policies, including the oil economy, that are promoting degradation of the world ecology and contribute to the decline of America as an Empire culture. This volume finally explores the factors pointing to the decline of the American Empire economy and imperial power and what to expect in the aftermath of American prominence and how to survive the decline while at the same time promoting policies and social-economic-religious-political changes that are needed in order to promote the emergence of a beneficial and sustainable culture. **$25.95soft** 1-884564-25-9, Hard Cover **$29.95soft** 1-884564-45-3

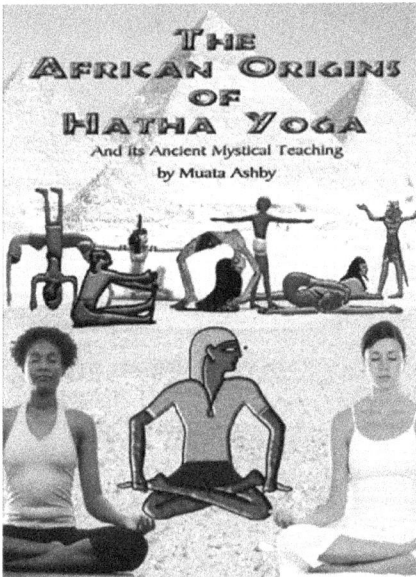

38. The African Origins of Hatha Yoga: And its Ancient Mystical Teaching

The subject of this present volume, The Ancient Egyptian Origins of Yoga Postures, formed one subject in the larger works, African Origins of Civilization Religion, Yoga Mysticism and Ethics Philosophy and the Book Egypt and India is the section of the book African Origins of Civilization. Those works contain the collection of all correlations between Ancient Egypt and India. This volume also contains some additional information not contained in the previous work. It was felt that this subject needed to be discussed more directly, being treated in one volume, as opposed to being contained in the larger work along with other subjects, because even in the early 21st century, the idea persists that the Yoga and specifically, Yoga Postures, were invented and developed only in India. The Ancient Egyptians were peoples originally from Africa who were, in ancient times, colonists in India. Therefore it is no surprise that many Indian traditions including religious and Yogic, would be found earlier in Ancient Egypt. Yet there is ample evidence from ancient writings and perhaps more importantly, iconographical evidences from the Ancient Egyptians themselves and the Indians themselves that prove the connection between Ancient Egypt and India as well as the existence of a discipline of Yoga Postures in Ancient Egypt long before its practice in India. This handy volume has been designed to be accessible to young adults and all others who would like to have an easy reference with documentation on this important subject. This is an important subject because the frame of reference with which we look at a culture depends strongly on our conceptions about its origins. In this case, if we look at the Ancient Egyptians as Asiatic peoples we would treat them and their culture in one way. If we see them as Africans we not only see them in a different light but we also must ascribe Africa with a glorious legacy that matches any other culture in human history. We would also look at the culture and philosophies of the Ancient Egyptians as having African insights instead of Asiatic ones. Those insights inform our knowledge bout other African traditions and we can also begin to understand in a deeper way the effect of Ancient Egyptian culture on African culture and also on the Asiatic as well. When we discover the deeper and more ancient practice of the postures system in Ancient Egypt that was called "Hatha Yoga" in India, we are able to find a new and expanded understanding of the practice that constitutes a discipline of spiritual practice that informs and revitalizes the Indian practices as well as all spiritual disciplines. $19.99 ISBN 1-884564-60-7

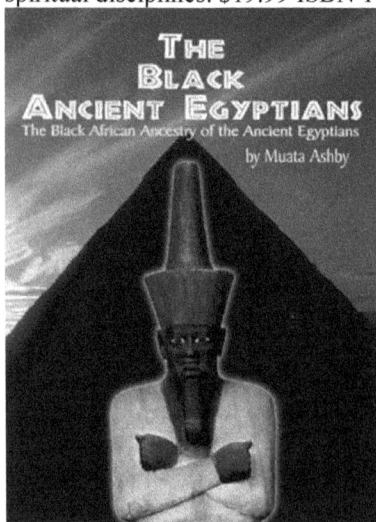

39. The Black Ancient Egyptians
This present volume, The Black Ancient Egyptians: The Black African Ancestry of the Ancient Egyptians, formed one subject in the larger

work: The African Origins of Civilization, Religion, Yoga Mysticism and Ethics Philosophy. It was felt that this subject needed to be discussed because even in the early 21st century, the idea persists that the Ancient Egyptians were peoples originally from Asia Minor who came into North-East Africa. Yet there is ample evidence from ancient writings and perhaps more importantly, iconographical evidences from the Ancient Egyptians themselves that proves otherwise. This handy volume has been designed to be accessible to young adults and all others who would like to have an easy reference with documentation on this important subject. This is an important subject because the frame of reference with which we look at a culture depends strongly on our conceptions about its origins. in this case, if we look at the Ancient Egyptians as Asiatic peoples we would treat them and their culture in one way. If we see them as Africans we not only see them in a different light but we also must ascribe Africa with a glorious legacy that matches any other culture in human history. We would also look at the culture and philosophies of the Ancient Egyptians as having African insights instead of Asiatic ones. Those insights inform our knowledge bout other African traditions and we can also begin to understand in a deeper way the effect of Ancient Egyptian culture on African culture and also on the Asiatic as well. ISBN 1-884564-21-6 $19.99

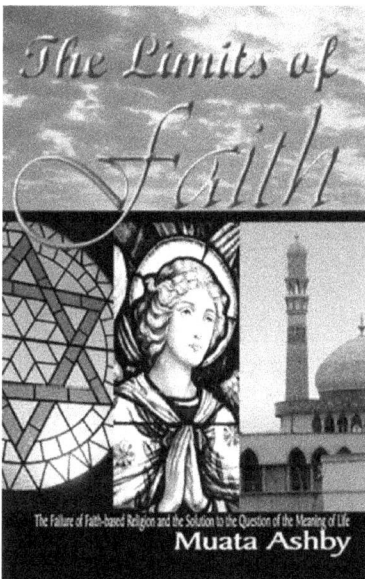

40. The Limits of Faith: The Failure of Faith-based Religions and the Solution to the Meaning of Life

Is faith belief in something without proof? And if so is there never to be any proof or discovery? If so what is the need of intellect? If faith is trust in something that is real is that reality historical, literal or metaphorical or philosophical? If knowledge is an essential element in faith why should there by so much emphasis on believing and not on understanding in the modern practice of religion? This volume is a compilation of essays related to the nature of religious faith in the context of its inception in human history as well as its meaning for religious practice and relations between religions in modern times. Faith has come to be regarded as a virtuous goal in life. However, many people have asked how can it be that an endeavor that is supposed to be dedicated to spiritual upliftment has led to more conflict in human history than any other social factor? ISBN 1884564631 SOFT COVER - $19.99, ISBN 1884564623 HARD COVER -$28.95

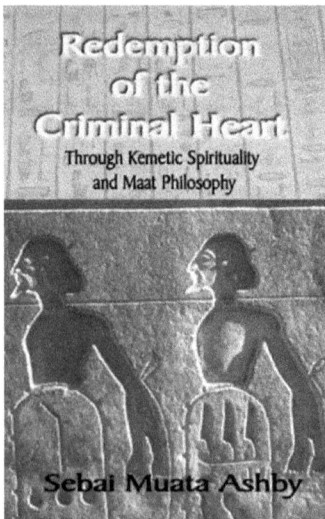

41. Redemption of The Criminal Heart Through Kemetic Spirituality and Maat Philosophy

Special book dedicated to inmates, their families and members of the Law Enforcement community. ISBN: 1-884564-70-4
$5.00

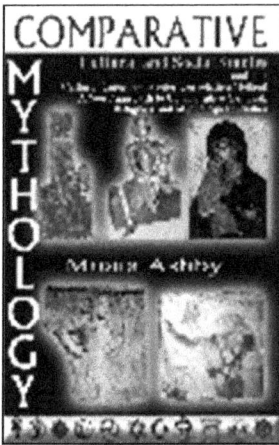

42. COMPARATIVE MYTHOLOGY

What are Myth and Culture and what is their importance for understanding the development of societies, human evolution and the search for meaning? What is the purpose of culture and how do cultures evolve? What are the elements of a culture and how can those elements be broken down and the constituent parts of a culture understood and compared? How do cultures interact? How does enculturation occur and how do people interact with other cultures? How do the processes of acculturation and cooptation occur and what does this mean for the development of a society? How can the study of myths and the elements of culture help in understanding the meaning of life and the means to promote understanding and peace in the world of human activity? This volume is the exposition of a method for studying and comparing cultures, myths and other social aspects of a society. It is an expansion on the Cultural Category Factor Correlation method for studying and comparing myths, cultures, religions and other aspects of human culture. It was originally introduced in the year 2002. This volume contains an expanded treatment as well as several refinements along with examples of the application of the method. the apparent. I hope you enjoy these art renditions as serene reflections of the mysteries of life. ISBN: 1-884564-72-0
Book price $21.95

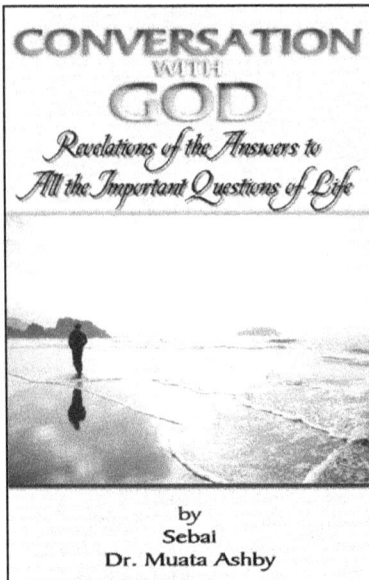

CONVERSATION
WITH
GOD
Revelations of the Answers to
All the Important Questions of Life

by
Sebai
Dr. Muata Ashby

43. CONVERSATION WITH GOD: Revelations of the Important Questions of Life
$24.99 U.S.

This volume contains a grouping of some of the questions that have been submitted to Sebai Dr. Muata Ashby. They are efforts by many aspirants to better understand and practice the teachings of mystical spirituality. It is said that when sages are asked spiritual questions they are relaying the wisdom of God, the Goddess, the Higher Self, etc. There is a very special quality about the Q & A process that does not occur during a regular lecture session. Certain points come out that would not come out otherwise due to the nature of the process which ideally occurs after a lecture. Having been to a certain degree enlightened by a lecture certain new questions arise and the answers to these have the effect of elevating the teaching of the lecture to even higher levels. Therefore, enjoy these exchanges and may they lead you to enlightenment, peace and prosperity. Available Late Summer 2007 ISBN: 1-884564-68-2

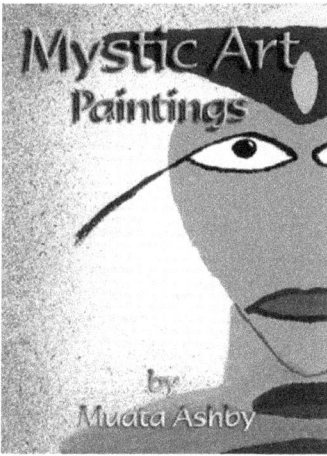

44. **MYSTIC ART PAINTINGS**

(with Full Color images) This book contains a collection of the small number of paintings that I have created over the years. Some were used as early book covers and others were done simply to express certain spiritual feelings; some were created for no purpose except to express the joy of color and the feeling of relaxed freedom. All are to elicit mystical awakening in the viewer. Writing a book on philosophy is like sculpture, the more the work is rewritten the reflections and ideas become honed and take form and become clearer and imbued with intellectual beauty. Mystic music is like meditation, a world of its own that exists about 1 inch above ground wherein the musician does not touch the ground. Mystic Graphic Art is meditation in form, color, image and reflected image which opens the door to the reality behind the apparent. I hope you enjoy these art renditions and my reflections on them as serene reflections of the mysteries of life, as visual renditions of the philosophy I have written about over the years. ISBN 1-884564-69-0 $19.95

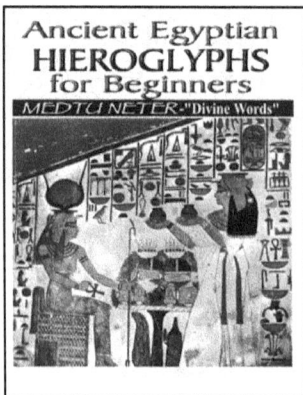

45. ANCIENT EGYPTIAN HIEROGLYPHS FOR BEGINNERS

This brief guide was prepared for those inquiring about how to enter into Hieroglyphic studies on their own at home or in study groups. First of all you should know that there are a few institutions around the world which teach how to read the Hieroglyphic text but due to the nature of the study there are perhaps only a handful of people who can read fluently. It is possible for anyone with average intelligence to achieve a high level of proficiency in reading inscriptions on temples and artifacts; however, reading extensive texts is another issue entirely. However, this introduction will give you entry into those texts if assisted by dictionaries and other aids. Most Egyptologists have a basic knowledge and keep dictionaries and notes handy when it comes to dealing with more difficult texts. Medtu Neter or the Ancient Egyptian hieroglyphic language has been considered as a "Dead Language." However, dead languages have always been studied by individuals who for the most part have taught themselves through various means. This book will discuss those means and how to use them most efficiently. ISBN 1884564429 **$28.95**

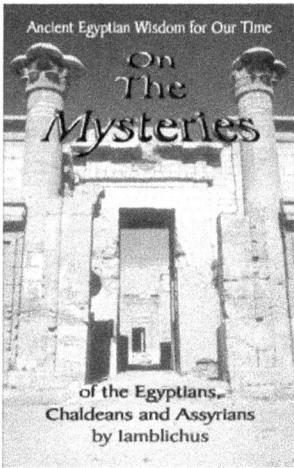

46. ON THE MYSTERIES: Wisdom of An Ancient Egyptian Sage
-with Foreword by Muata Ashby
This volume, On the Mysteries, by Iamblichus (Abamun) is a unique form or scripture out of the Ancient Egyptian religious tradition. It is written in a form that is not usual or which is not usually found in the remnants of Ancient Egyptian scriptures. It is in the form of teacher and disciple, much like the Eastern scriptures such as Bhagavad Gita or the Upanishads. This form of writing may not have been necessary in Ancient times, because the format of teaching in Egypt was different prior to the conquest period by the Persians, Assyrians, Greeks and later the Romans. The question and answer format can be found but such extensive discourses and corrections of misunderstandings within the context of a teacher - disciple relationship is not usual. It therefore provides extensive insights into the times when it was written and the state of practice of Ancient Egyptian and other mystery religions. This has important implications for our times because we are today, as in the Greco-Roman period, also besieged with varied religions and new age philosophies as well as social strife and war. How can we understand our times and also make sense of the forest of spiritual traditions? How can we cut through the cacophony of religious fanaticism, and ignorance as well as misconceptions about the mysteries on the other in order to discover the true purpose of religion and the secret teachings that open up the mysteries of life and the way to enlightenment and immortality? This book, which comes to us from so long ago, offers us transcendental wisdom that applied to the world two thousand years ago as well as our world today. ISBN 1-884564-64-X $25.95

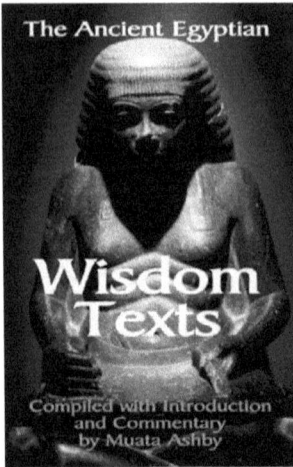

47. The Ancient Egyptian Wisdom Texts -Compiled by Muata Ashby

The Ancient Egyptian Wisdom Texts are a genre of writings from the ancient culture that have survived to the present and provide a vibrant record of the practice of spiritual evolution otherwise known as religion or yoga philosophy in Ancient Egypt. The principle focus of the Wisdom Texts is the cultivation of understanding, peace, harmony, selfless service, self-control, Inner fulfillment and spiritual realization. When these factors are cultivated in human life, the virtuous qualities in a human being begin to manifest and sinfulness, ignorance and negativity diminish until a person is able to enter into higher consciousness, the coveted goal of all civilizations. It is this virtuous mode of life which opens the door to self-discovery and spiritual enlightenment. Therefore, the Wisdom Texts are important scriptures on the subject of human nature, spiritual psychology and mystical philosophy. The teachings presented in the Wisdom Texts form the foundation of religion as well as the guidelines for conducting the affairs of every area of social interaction including commerce, education, the army, marriage, and especially the legal system. These texts were sources for the famous 42 Precepts of Maat of the Pert M Heru (Book of the Dead), essential regulations of good conduct to develop virtue and purity in order to attain higher consciousness and immortality after death. ISBN1-884564-65-8 $18.95

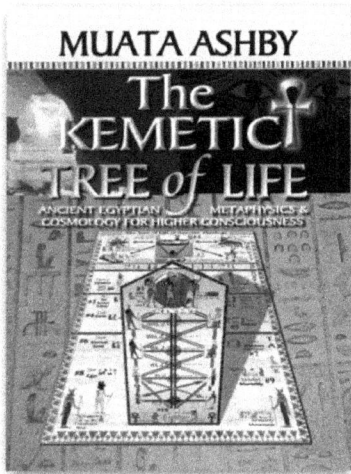

48. THE KEMETIC TREE OF LIFE
THE KEMETIC TREE OF LIFE: Newly Revealed Ancient Egyptian Cosmology and Metaphysics for Higher Consciousness
The Tree of Life is a roadmap of a journey which explains how Creation came into being and how it will end. It also explains what Creation is composed of and also what human beings are and what they are composed of. It also explains the process of Creation, how Creation develops, as well as who created Creation and where that entity may be found. It also explains how a human being may discover that entity and in so doing also discover the secrets of Creation, the meaning of life and the means to break free from the pathetic condition of human limitation and mortality in order to discover the higher realms of being by discovering the principles, the levels of existence that are beyond the simple physical and material aspects of life. This book contains color plates **ISBN: 1-884564-74-7**
$27.95 U.S.

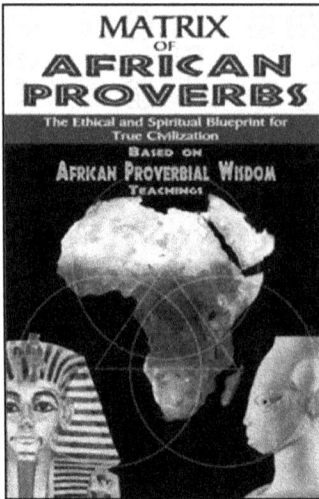

49-MATRIX OF AFRICAN PROVERBS: The Ethical and Spiritual Blueprint

This volume sets forth the fundamental principles of African ethics and their practical applications for use by individuals and organizations seeking to model their ethical policies using the Traditional African values and concepts of ethical human behavior for the proper sustenance and management of society. Furthermore, this book will provide guidance as to how the Traditional African Ethics may be viewed and applied, taking into consideration the technological and social advancements in the present. This volume also presents the principles of ethical culture, and references for each to specific injunctions from Traditional African Proverbial Wisdom Teachings. These teachings are compiled from varied Pre-colonial African societies including Yoruba, Ashanti, Kemet, Malawi, Nigeria, Ethiopia, Galla, Ghana and many more. ISBN 1-884564-77-1

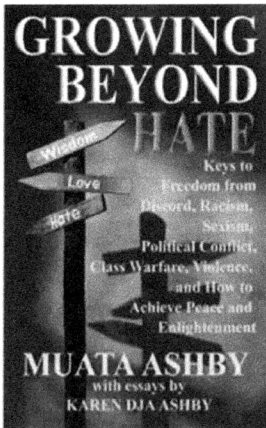

50- **Growing Beyond Hate: Keys to Freedom from Discord, Racism, Sexism, Political Conflict, Class Warfare, Violence, and How to Achieve Peace and Enlightenment**---INTRODUCTION: WHY DO WE HATE? Hatred is one of the fundamental motivating aspects of human life; the other is desire. Desire can be of a worldly nature or of a spiritual, elevating nature. Worldly desire and hatred are like two sides of the same coin in that human life is usually swaying from one to the other; but the question is why? And is there a way to satisfy the desiring or hating mind in such a way as to find peace in life? Why do human beings go to war? Why do human beings perpetrate violence against one another? And is there a way not just to understand the phenomena but to resolve the issues that plague humanity and could lead to a more harmonious society? Hatred is perhaps the greatest scourge of humanity in that it leads to misunderstanding, conflict and untold miseries of life and clashes between individuals, societies and nations. Therefore, the riddle of Hatred, that is, understanding the sources of it and how to confront, reduce and even eradicate it so as to bring forth the fulfillment in life and peace for society, should be a top priority for social scientists, spiritualists and philosophers. This book is written from the perspective of spiritual philosophy based on the mystical wisdom and sema or yoga philosophy of the Ancient Egyptians. This philosophy, originated and based in the wisdom of Shetaut Neter, the Egyptian Mysteries, and Maat, ethical way of life in society and in spirit, contains Sema-Yogic wisdom and understanding of life's predicaments that can allow a human being of any ethnic group to understand and overcome the causes of hatred, racism, sexism, violence and disharmony in life, that plague human society. ISBN: 1-884564-81-X

www.ingramcontent.com/pod-product-compliance
Lightning Source LLC
Chambersburg PA
CBHW050727030426
42336CB00012B/1450